THE BEST HITS ON ROUTE 66

THE BEST HITS ON

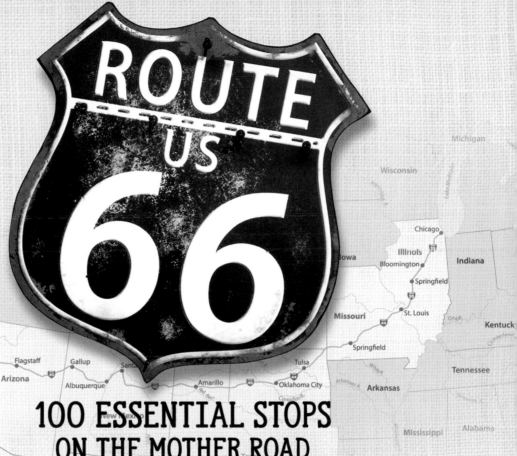

100 ESSENTIAL STOPS
ON THE MOTHER ROAD

AMY BIZZARRI

Globe
Pequot

Guilford, Connecticut

Globe
Pequot

An imprint of The Rowman & Littlefield Publishing Group, Inc.
4501 Forbes Blvd., Ste. 200
Lanham, MD 20706
www.rowman.com

Distributed by NATIONAL BOOK NETWORK

British Library Cataloguing in Publication Information available

Library of Congress Cataloging-in-Publication Data available

ISBN 978-1-4930-3690-5 (paperback)

ISBN 978-1-4930-3691-2 (e-book)

∞™ The paper used in this publication meets the minimum requirements of American National Standard for Information Sciences—Permanence of Paper for Printed Library Materials, ANSI/NISO Z39.48-1992

Printed in the United States of America

For Daniel and Chiara:

May you always take the high road, keep your cool even on the bumpiest of roads,

focus on the beauty that is everywhere if we seek it, and always, always cherish

the memories we made along Route 66 during the summer of 2018.

Love, Mom

CONTENTS

Highway 66 is the main migrant road. 66—the long concrete path across the country, waving gently up and down on the map, from Mississippi to Bakersfield—over the red lands and the grey lands, twisting up into the mountains, crossing the Divide and down into the bright and terrible desert, and across the desert to the mountains again, and into the rich California valleys. 66 is the path of a people in flight, refugees from dust and shrinking land, from the thunder of tractors and shrinking ownership, from the desert's slow northward invasion, from the twisting winds that howl up out of Texas, from the floods that bring no richness to the land and steal what little richness is there. From all of these the people are in flight, and they come into 66 from the tributary side roads, from the wagon tracks and the rutted country roads. 66 is the mother road, the road of flight.

John Steinbeck, *The Grapes of Wrath*

ICON KEY

 Activity

 Sightseeing

 Food

 Accommodations

Shopping

INTRODUCTION:
AMERICA'S MAIN STREET

It's America's most cherished byway, stretching over 2,400 miles from Chicago to Santa Monica. Countless motorists have rambled along the "double six," stopping to pay homage to the stunning natural landscapes, important historical landmarks, and iconic as well as just plain wacky roadside attractions. As Route 66 approaches its 100th birthday, there's no better time to set off on a Mother Road journey of your very own.

The Best Hits on Route 66: 100 Essential Stops on the Mother Road makes it easier than ever to plan your epic adventure. With thousands of sights to see in the eight states and three time zones traversed via the byway, this comprehensive checklist filters out the frivolous and focuses on the quintessential, so you can plan your road trip with ease. Specialized, themed itineraries will help you make the most of your time frame. Inspiring and practical, this is the premier guide to all the famous . . . and off-the-radar . . . stops along America's Mother Road that you simply must not miss.

As in life, it's not the destination that matters but rather the beautiful vistas, new friends, and even the bumps in the road you encounter along the way. Here's to many magical moments on the Mother Road and memories to last a lifetime!

–**Amy Bizzarri**

City of Kingman

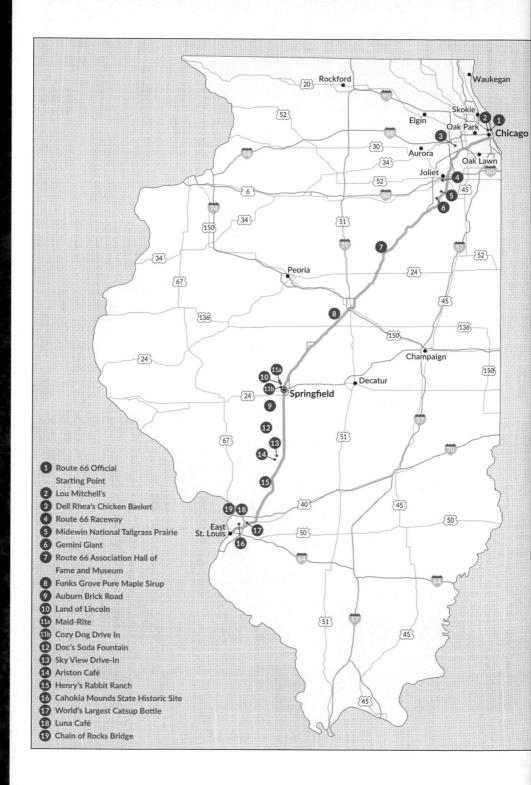

ILLINOIS

1. Route 66 Official Starting Point
2. Lou Mitchell's
3. Dell Rhea's Chicken Basket
4. Route 66 Raceway
5. Midewin National Tallgrass Prairie
6. Gemini Giant
7. Route 66 Association Hall of Fame and Museum
8. Funks Grove Pure Maple Sirup
9. Auburn Brick Road
10. Land of Lincoln
11a. Maid-Rite
11b. Cozy Dog Drive In
12. Doc's Soda Fountain
13. Sky View Drive-In
14. Ariston Café
15. Henry's Rabbit Ranch
16. Cahokia Mounds State Historic Site
17. World's Largest Catsup Bottle
18. Luna Café
19. Chain of Rocks Bridge

1. Route 66 Official Starting Point and the Ledge of the Willis Tower Skydeck *Chicago, IL*

2. Lou Mitchell's Restaurant and Bakery *Chicago, IL*

3. Dell Rhea's Chicken Basket *Willowbrook, IL*

4. Car Racing Experience at the Route 66 Raceway *Elwood, IL*

5. Buffalo Roaming at Midewin National Tallgrass Prairie *Wilmington, IL*

6. Gemini Giant *Wilmington, IL*

7. Bob Waldmire's 1972 VW Microbus at the Route 66 Association Hall of Fame and Museum *Pontiac, IL*

8. Funks Grove Pure Maple Sirup *Shirley, IL*

9. Auburn Brick Road *Auburn, IL*

10. Land of Lincoln *Springfield, IL*

11. Springfield's Iconic Diners *Springfield, IL*

12. Doc's Soda Fountain *Girard, IL*

13. Sky View Drive-In *Litchfield, IL*

14. Ariston Café *Litchfield, IL*

15. Henry's Rabbit Ranch *Stauton, IL*

16. World's Largest Catsup Bottle *Collinsville, IL*

17. Cahokia Mounds State Historic Site *Collinsville, IL*

18. Luna Café *Granite City, IL*

19. Chain of Rocks Bridge *Granite City, IL /St. Louis, MO*

ROUTE 66 OFFICIAL STARTING POINT AND THE LEDGE OF THE WILLIS TOWER SKYDECK ⑯

Your adventure of a lifetime begins here, in the midst of downtown Chicago's hustle and bustle. An official US 66 sign, mounted so that it faces westbound traffic, marks the Mother Road's starting point on East Adams Street, just west of its intersection with South Michigan Avenue.

Route 66, however, originally began on Jackson Boulevard at Michigan Avenue.

Early 1920s Chicago boasted one of the largest street railway systems in the world, but Jackson Street remained one of the few downtown boulevards without a streetcar line, making it the perfect pick for a new, transnational US highway. Officially named Route 66 on April 30, 1926, Jackson Boulevard became part of the Mother Road and began whisking generations of migrants and road-tripping vacationers westward. In 1955, however, the boulevard was transformed into a one-way street, and Adams Street at Michigan Avenue became the new launching point for US-66.

At 1,450 feet high—1,730 feet if you include its twin antenna towers—Willis Tower is the second tallest building in North America and the twelfth tallest building in the world. Completed in 1973, the former Sears Tower was built to house Sears, Roebuck & Co, once the largest retailer in the world. The tower's thrilling observation deck, the Skydeck, is the highest in the United States. On a clear day, you can see up to 50 miles

PIT STOP PHOTO OP

Snap a selfie in front of the official starting point sign on East Adams Street and then make your way skyward to the best place to kick off your Route 66 adventure: 1,353 feet in the sky above Jackson Boulevard.

down Route 66; looking to the east you can see across Lake Michigan, all the way to Indiana and Michigan.

Even the elevator ride up to the top of the tower is a thrill. The ride only takes about 60 seconds, and you'll feel the pressure as you rise toward the clouds. On a windy day, you'll also feel the sway: The tower is known to move about 8 inches at the top on remarkably "Windy City" days.

For the ultimate look at the road ahead, step upon the Ledge, a panel of four glass balconies extending 4 feet from the west-facing façade of the 103rd floor, and peer through the glass floor at Route 66, which lies 1,353 feet below. Though standing on the glass is enough to give even the bravest of souls a scare, these panels can bear 5 tons of weight, so you can count on not falling over—or through—the Ledge.

Route 66 Official Starting Point, East Adams Street, just west of its intersection with South Michigan Avenue, Chicago

Ledge of the Willis Tower Skydeck, 233 S. Wacker Dr., Chicago, IL; (312) 875-9447; theskydeck.com

Courtesy of Illinois Office of Tourism

LOU MITCHELL'S RESTAURANT AND BAKERY

Lou Mitchell's has been providing the fuel—a.k.a. the "world's best coffee"—for Route 66 adventures since the highway first opened for business in 1926. As the first full-service restaurant and bakery you'll encounter along West Jackson Boulevard, the first westbound tract of the Mother Road, it has long served as a place of beginnings, giving patrons the gas they need for the road trip of a lifetime . . . or just another day at the office.

If you're especially hungry for a hearty breakfast, the line outside this iconic Chicago diner seems to stretch down the route all the way to Santa Monica Pier. Don't let the mouthwatering smell of pancakes and maple syrup overcome you; keep your eyes peeled for the hostess who passes out doughnut holes and Milk Duds to waiting customers.

Though the city that surrounds it has grown tall with skyscrapers over the years, little has changed inside: The original wooden stools at the multisided counters are packed with coffee-sipping, newspaper-reading regulars; couples cozy up to the wooden two-seater booths; families share laughter over fluffy pancakes in the larger booths. The shiny silver toasters pop up slices of bread ripe for a generous spread of butter; the salty-sweet smell of bacon wafts through the air; servers swerve from table to table, gracefully balancing fresh-from-the-skillet omelets and steaming coffee pots.

Lou Mitchell's has been a long-standing whistle stop on the campaign trails of many political hopefuls, and the eclectic clientele also makes it a prime source for popular opinion when media outlets want to know how tried-and-true Chicagoans really feel about an issue or a candidate. Sit at the counter, where you can best trade travel tips with both fellow Route 66 road trippers about to set off into the sunrise or just swinging into town from an east-to-west journey.

Most everything here is made in-house, daily, from the bismarcks to the Belgian malted waffles. The cinnamon twists are hand rolled and the OJ freshly squeezed from Florida oranges. Lou Mitchell's serves uniquely double-yolked eggs, and you can order them any way you'd like; the omelets here are big enough for two and available in 20-plus savory combinations. Even the orange marmalade—which you'll always find on the table—is prepared the old-fashioned way and canned in the kitchen. The soda jerk on staff still whips up chocolate phosphates and Chicago egg creams using the same recipes from the diner's early days. If you're traveling with little ones, the Mitchell Mouse pancake—a mouse-shaped pancake with whipped cream eyebrows and smile, Milk Dud eyes, and a maraschino cherry nose—is always

> **Foodie Find**
>
> ## THE WORLD'S BEST CUP OF COFFEE
>
> Lou Mitchell's has been providing the fuel—a.k.a. the "world's best coffee"—for Route 66 adventures since the highway first opened for business in 1926.

a delight. Lou Mitchell's is the only diner in the world that always serves dessert after breakfast: a scoop of creamy vanilla ice cream to cleanse the palate.

Be sure to take a cup of the "world's best" coffee to go and plan on loosening your belt a few notches before you hit the road.

565 W. Jackson Blvd., Chicago, IL; (312) 939-3111; loumitchellsrestaurant.com

DELL RHEA'S CHICKEN BASKET 🍴

In the early years of Route 66, Ervin "Irv" Kolarik's served up sandwiches to entice customers to his humble Route 66 gas station. Sometime around 1938, two local ladies made him a deal he couldn't refuse: They would share their top-secret recipe for the most delectable fried chicken in the world if in return he promised to purchase chickens from their family farms. Irv signed on the dotted line, and the Dell Rhea's Chicken Basket empire, originally National Chicken Basket, was born.

Crispy with a tangy buttermilk bite, rumors of the best fried chicken on the planet spread quickly among Route 66's most frequent travelers. Before long, the line stretched out the door. When it was designated an official bus stop for the Los Angeles–bound Blue

Courtesy of Illinois Office of Tourism

Bird Bus Line, business boomed as patrons knew they could buy both a basket of delicious fried chicken and a ticket out of town. Kolarik saw such success as a restaurateur that he ditched his gas station business, transforming the two auto repair garages into dining rooms and adding a one-story brick restaurant and lounge. From the restaurant's large front windows, guests enjoyed watching airplanes landing and taking off at the small airport once located just across the street. Dell Rhea's was a place of departures and arrivals, all commemorated with mouthwatering chicken.

Then came Interstate-55, which stole Route 66's traffic and, in turn, the National Chicken Basket's customers. The bank took possession of the property. In 1963, Chicago hotelier Delbert "Dell" Rhea and his wife, Grace, bought the restaurant for a bargain-basement price.

Today the main dining room clucks with farm-style ambience thanks to the many ceramic roosters and hens that line the glass and wood canted windowsills. In the wintertime, diners gather around the roaring fireplace.

The Chicken Basket stands as the perennial favorite menu item. It takes a half-hour minimum from order to table, but this only means that you can count on finger-lickin', freshly battered and fried chicken, served up in a basket. It's easy to fill up on the oven-fresh buttermilk biscuits alone, which are served warm, in a basket, with honey and butter, upon arrival.

The beloved restaurant's neon sign "Dell Rhea, Chicken Basket, Cocktail Lounge" was recently restored thanks to a grant from the National Park Service and the Illinois Scenic Byway Association by David Hutson of Neon Times in St. Charles, Missouri.

645 Joliet Rd., Willowbrook, IL; (630) 325-0780; chickenbasket.com

CAR RACING EXPERIENCE AT THE ROUTE 66 RACEWAY

Dreaming of putting your pedal to the metal and driving off into the sunset . . . at full speed . . . along Route 66? Drag racing dreams come true at the Route 66 Raceway in Joliet, Illinois, where the Race Your Ride experience gives guests the chance to set off on the same track as the quarter-mile legends. If you want to see if you have what it takes to become the next John Force, this is a don't-miss Mother Road adventure.

Founded in 1998, the Route 66 Raceway is the first official stadium dedicated to drag racing in the US. Its quarter-mile concrete-and-asphalt drag strip is owned and operated by the International Speedway Corporation and is the small sister track to the 1.5-mile tri-oval Chicagoland Speedway, also located in Joliet and host to the NASCAR Sprint Cup. This one-of-a-kind raceway hosts weekly professional drag races and demolition derbies, including the ET Bracket Series racing, NHRA Jr. Drag Racing, the World of Outlaws, and NHRA Mello Yello Drag Racing series.

Race Your Ride is considered a "Test & Tune," an opportunity to safely see how fast you can race down the dragstrip in your own street-legal vehicle. Open to everyone from first-time racers in mom-style minivans to seasoned veterans with souped-up dragsters, the only initial requirement is that all race-ready cars and motorcycles must pass the NHRA Technical Inspection to participate. There is no limit on the age of participating automobiles, so feel free to kick your '57 Chevy back into gear. Your driving skills won't be tested pre-race, but of course you'll need a valid driver's license. Copilots are a no-go, but they are welcome to cheer you on from the 30,000-seat grandstand that surrounds the starting line.

Being able to read a "Christmas Tree" is another racing requirement. This system of colorful, merry lights lets a racer know when to stop, when to go, and when to watch out. The top four bulbs are the "Pre-Stage" lights that let the driver and opponent know they're almost to the starting line and nearing the start of the race. When the "Stage" lights shine bright, officials know that racers are ready and in position to begin. Finally, the flash of the green light signals that it's time to shake your tail feathers to the finish line.

3200 S. Chicago St., Joliet, IL; (855) 794-7223; route66raceway.com

BUFFALO ROAMING AT MIDEWIN NATIONAL TALLGRASS PRAIRIE ⓰

If you could turn back the clock 300 years, you'd likely encounter a massive, thundering herd of American buffalo, a.k.a. bison, at some point along your Route 66 journey across the US. More than 30 million buffalo roamed the North American plains upon the arrival of the first Europeans; but by the early 1800s, these shaggy, humped herbivores faced extinction due to overhunting and habitat destruction. While they once roamed Illinois in vast numbers, the last bison in Illinois was killed in 1837, and most of the tallgrass prairie land they had grazed upon had been converted to farmland. Of the 21 million acres of tallgrass prairie that once stretched across Illinois, today only .01% remains.

There is still one spot in Illinois where beloved buffalo can roam the beautiful plains in peace. At Midewin National Tallgrass Prairie, the largest conservation site in the Chicagoland area and the only federal tallgrass prairie preserve east of the Mississippi River, an experimental herd of *Bison bison*, introduced in the fall of 2015, now munch, wild and free, on the prairie plants.

Wikimedia Commons

The history of the Midewin National Tallgrass Prairie reaches all the way back to the 1600s, when the Potawatomi Indians, as well as smaller numbers of Ottawa, Ojibwa, and other Native American tribes, called this corner of Illinois home. They considered the buffalo a sacred animal and religious symbol, and every part of the animal was put to use: hides were transformed into clothing and tipi covers, sinews were used for sewing, bones became arrows. The prairie was named Midewin (pronounced *mi-DAY-win*) after the eponymous Grand Medicine Society of the Anishinaabeg, a sacred society of Native American healers once entrusted with keeping the greater Anishinaabe society, which included the Potawatomi, in balance.

In 1940, the prairie and surrounding farmland became the site of the Joliet Army Ammunition Plant, a large arsenal that produced the ammunition used in World War II and the Korean and Vietnam Wars. The Midewin National Tallgrass Prairie was established by in 1996 thanks to the Illinois Land Conservation Act, which transferred 19,165 acres of the US Army–held land to the US Department of Agriculture's Forest Service. The intensive cleanup that followed included controlled explosions of live explosive cartridges that were heard up to 3 miles away.

In 2015, a herd of 27 bison was introduced to the new digs. The 4 bulls from Colorado and 23 cows from South Dakota found the time for romance on the plains, and by late spring 2017, baby calves, born bright orange in color, had increased the size of the herd to around 50.

Start your visit at the Midewin Welcome Center, where exhibits on glaciers, prairie habitats, and wildlife highlight the natural history of the land. Docents are on hand to direct you to the grazing buffalo. The 34 miles of trails wind through scenic vistas that showcase what Illinois looked like before the arrival of French explorers Jacques Marquette and Louis Jolliet in 1673.

Not up for taking a hike? On a guided Auto Caravan Tour, you can drive your own car while listening to your guide via a provided handheld radio. You'll make a number of stops along the way with only short walks to points of interest.

30239 S. State Route 53, Wilmington, IL; (815) 423-6370; fs.usda.gov/main/midewin/home

GEMINI GIANT ⊙

He stands tall, greeting the westbound Route 66 traffic flowing through this eastern entrance to Wilmington, Illinois, ready for takeoff, rocket in hand, slick, deep sea-foam green jumpsuit, welding mask . . . *err* . . . space helmet in place. The Gemini Giant is a man who knew that changing with the times was a means to not only survive but thrive. Built to advertise a common car part, he ditched his muffler and transformed it into a moon-bound ship at the peak of the mid-century space race.

Once upon a time, the Gemini Giant was one of many oversize statues that advertised everything from auto parts to axes. The times changed, but many of those men didn't, their jobs outsourced by billboards and radio and television commercials. The Gemini Giant adapted, becoming a symbol of the advancing technological age.

Likewise, Wilmington, the Gemini Giant's riverside home-town, learned to change with the times, too. The first settlers to the area took advantage of the Kankakee River's might and built one of the first grist mills in the region, in the 1830s. Farmers traveled from near and far to have their wheat and corn ground at the mill. The Eagle Hotel (100 Water St.), which sprang up in 1836, hosted farmers, stagecoach travelers, and, eventually, Route 66 road trippers when the high-way was inaugurated in 1926. (Sadly, the oldest hotel on Route 66 suffered a fire and is not able to be visited at the moment, though it is currently being restored by the Wilmington Area Historical Society.) Today the town boasts industry giants Dow and US Cold Storage as major employers.

The Gemini Giant's ancestry is tied to the diner he guards from the parking lot. When it opened in the late 1950s, it was a Dairy Delight. Owners John and Bernice Korelc capitalized on moon mania

Courtesy of Illinois Office of Tourism

by renaming it the Launching Pad in 1965. At a restaurant convention, they discovered a Muffler Man that, once transformed into a Gemini space program participant, became the unmissable giant, capturing potential customers along the byway.

Further west down Route 66, Wilmington is home the Gemini Giant's brother from another era. A forest-green brontosaurus grazes atop the former Sinclair Gas Station, now a tire repair shop, at 201 E. Baltimore St. One of many marketing icons born of the Sinclair Oil Company in the 1930s, this 80-pound fiberglass monster is one of the few that didn't meet the fate of extinction.

810 E. Baltimore St., Wilmington, IL

BOB WALDMIRE'S 1972 VW MICROBUS AT THE ROUTE 66 ASSOCIATION HALL OF FAME AND MUSEUM 🔘

Legendary artist and cartographer Bob Waldmire found his hippie home on Route 66. For 40 years, he lived his version of the American dream: an itinerant lifestyle along the route, where his family of fellow wanderers gathered at small-town diner counters. He discovered his wealth in his friendships and freedom. As the unofficial Route 66 ambassador, his iconic images and intricate maps captured America's byway of yesteryear; his artistic talent gave him the utter independence he craved.

"The main reason I became a traveling artist was to avoid having a real job," he told the *Chicago Tribune* shortly before his death in 2009. "It was about being free to move. Wanderlust."

Born in St. Louis, Missouri, Waldmire grew up in Springfield, Illinois, where his father, Ed, inventor of the corn dog, owned the Cozy Dog Diner, located on the original Route 66. From his dad's diner, Waldmire was inspired by the comings and goings of Mother Road travelers who shared their adventures over coffee and cozy dogs. A 1962 family road trip to California sealed his lifelong goal: Though he briefly homesteaded in Arizona and even reopened the vintage 1934 Hackberry General Store in the ghost

town of Hackberry, Arizona, as a Route 66 tourism information stop and souvenir shop, Waldmire made the road his home, rambling to and fro on Route 66 aboard his VW microbus and later a yellow school bus that he converted into an extraordinary home/library/art gallery and christened the "Road Yacht."

You can find several souvenirs of Bob Waldmire's life on the route in Pontiac, Illinois, the historic, Livingston County town traversed by Route 66. The don't-miss Route 66 Hall of Fame and Museum is home to two prized Waldmire artifacts. Perhaps the most beloved is his orange 1972 Volkswagen microbus, which not only was Waldmire's home as he traveled from stop to stop, selling his intricate Mother Road–inspired drawings along the way to earn his keep on the road, but also the inspiration for the hippie character Fillmore from the 2006 Pixar animated motion picture *Cars*.

Like Fillmore, who has a sticker on his rear end that indicates "I brake for Jackalopes," Waldmire was an extreme animal lover and vegan, known for warning his fellow travelers to be attentive of wildlife along the route. Pixar originally planned on naming the character Waldmire, but the real-life Waldmire stood firm to his vegetarian principals and declined, even though it meant he would lose out on trademarked earnings.

He refused to be affiliated with toys bearing his name tucked into McDonald's Happy Meals, meat-laden fast food marketed to children.

And just like his inspiration Waldmire, who many considered the last tried-and-true hippie to grace the planet, Fillmore is a fan of Jimi Hendrix, embraces alternative energy, and fuels up with marijuana: Check out Waldmire's personal stash, kept in the two mysterious boxes slung under the VW van. Whenever police pulled him over, he was quick to note that they were nests for his pet snakes. Waldmire's bus is fitted with a solar panel for auxiliary power and decorated with organic and colorful elements that give it a zany yet homey vibe.

Though the quirky VW is the highlight of the museum, over 1,000 artifacts and pictures on display delve into the history of Route 66 in Illinois and include many of the artist's representative works dating all the way back to his teenage years.

Head to the rear of the museum where you'll find Waldmire's upgraded highway home, the Inventive Road Yacht. Once a yellow school bus and now a mansion on wheels, the yacht features two levels of living space, a hand-built sauna, compostable toilet, rainwater collection system, solar panels, a wood stove for heat, and a second-floor back porch, perfect for soaking in wide western vistas.

Pontiac, Illinois, is also home to a wonderful collection of murals depicting the city's history, painted by the Walldogs, a collective of 150 sign painters and muralists who

PIT STOP PHOTO OP

The world's largest mural of a Route 66 sign, located next to the Road Yacht at the Route 66 Association Hall of Fame and Museum, also features a small segment of original Route 66 pavement bricks: You're welcome to park your car here for a classic souvenir photo. (Access to the mural is from Main Street in the 300 block, just off of Howard Street, IL Route 116.)

arrived on the scene in the summer of 2009, painting 18 magnificent murals in just four days.

Bob Waldmire's last commissioned mural project, a 66-foot-long map of the entire length of Route 66, is stretched out on a brick wall near the corner of Madison and Howard Streets. Waldmire died before he was able to complete the project, but more than 500 of his friends gathered to paint the final touches in his honor in 2011. His ashes were spread along the route, making him a perpetual part of the historic highway he so treasured.

110 W. Howard St., Pontiac, IL; (815) 844-4566; il66assoc.org/destination/route-66-association-hall-of-fame-museum

FUNKS GROVE PURE MAPLE SIRUP

Pancakes and maple syrup are a match made in American heaven, and Funks Grove, Illinois, is a town dedicated to the sticky, sweet sap.

The native Illini were the first to recognize the sap of the sugar maple trees that lined the banks of Timber Creek as a source of nutrition, energy, and delightful sweetness. Every year, in the late winter months, when freezing and thawing temperatures caused the sap to run, they set off to harvest the prized sap, using stone tools to make V-shaped cuts into the trees' trunks to access the stored starch, inserting reeds or pieces of bark, and drawing the golden liquid out into buckets made of birch bark. Hot cooking stones were dropped into the buckets to reduce and thicken the sap into syrup.

In 1824, pioneer rancher Isaac Funk traveled to the area from Kentucky. The excellent water supply, fertile soil, and abundance of trees led him to stay and establish his livestock empire. Funk found great success despite setbacks, eventually serving in the Illinois Senate, where he befriended Abraham Lincoln. At first the Funk family harvested

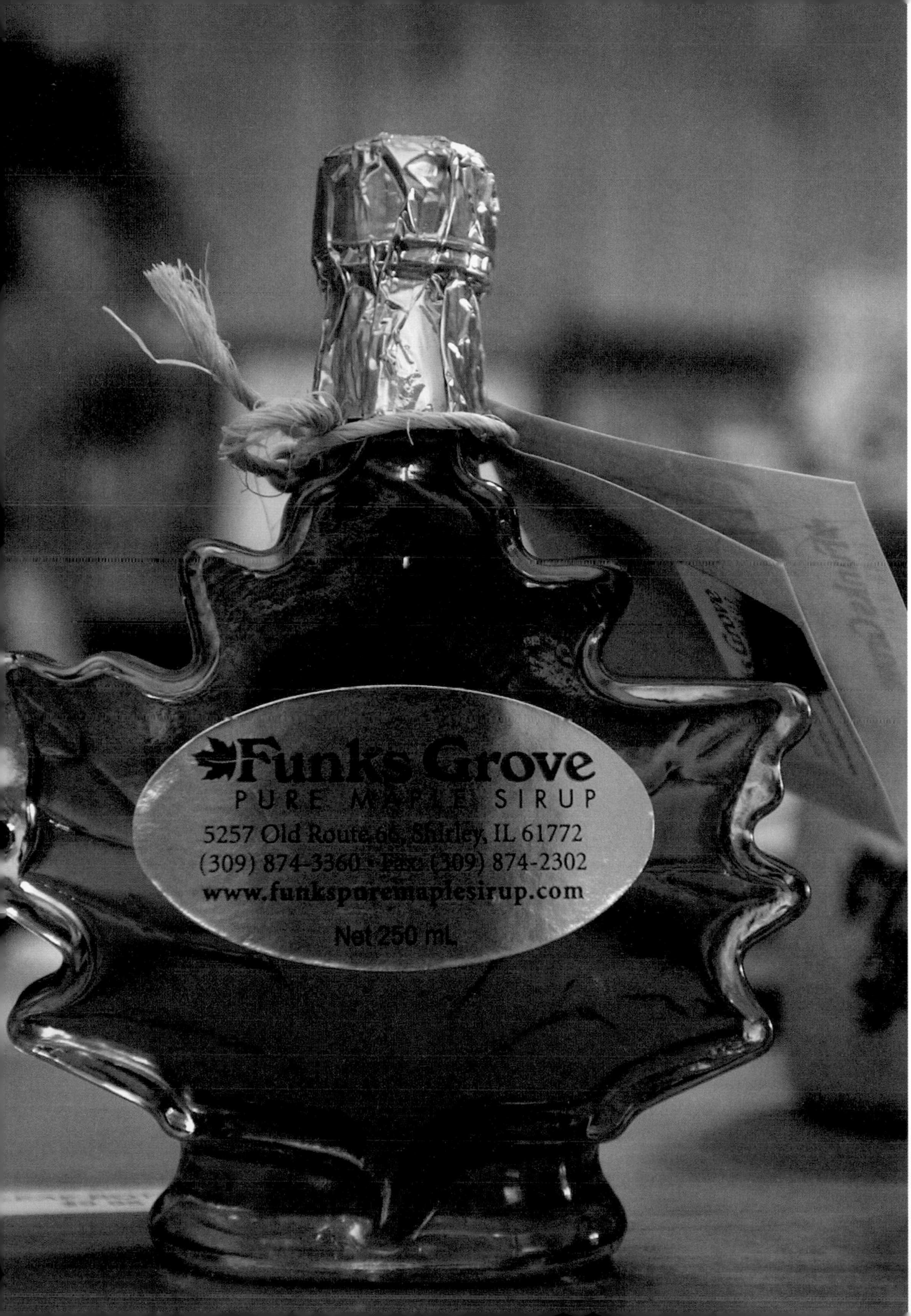

Courtesy of Illinois Office of Tourism

their sap for personal use, but by 1891, Isaac's grandson, Arthur, began selling the syrup commercially.

To this day, the sticky business remains in the Funk family, though production has increased to over 7,000 spouts, or "taps," placed in the over 3,000 sugar maple trees that have shared their bounty for generations upon generations. At the family's small shop, visitors stock up on syrup, which is sold in half-gallon jugs as well as smaller, table-ready, leaf-shape glass bottles.

Foodie Find

FUNKS GROVE'S MAPLE SIRUP LEAF CANDY

Plastic tubing and vacuum pumps have replaced reed siphons, and today the sap is boiled to remove the water. It takes up to 50 gallons of sap to make just 1 gallon of the precious amber syrup, and the Funk family produces only a little under 2,000 gallons each year, making it one of the most cherished foodie finds along Route 66.

For the record, the "sirup" spelling isn't a typo: It's a tribute to Hazel Funk Holmes, who ran syrup production in the 1920s and '30s. Holmes was savvy enough to place Funk family timber and farmland in a trust that would protect it for future generations, while also quirkily expressing her wish that "sirup" be spelled with an "i." Thanks to her efforts, Funks Grove is the largest remaining intact prairie grove in the state of Illinois and portions have been designated a National Natural Landmark by the US Department of Interior.

5257 Old Route 66, Shirley, IL; (309) 874-3360; funksmaplesirup.com

AUBURN BRICK ROAD 📷

Route 66 stretches across Illinois peacefully and evenly, passing through prairie and farmland that stretches on for miles, connecting small town to small town. It wasn't until

1938 that the entire route was officially paved, making a trip from start to end an altogether smoother ride.

Though not all of Route 66 was paved by the time it was commissioned in 1926, the two-lane byway in Illinois boasted mostly smooth, paved "modern" roads from Chicago to St. Louis, thanks to infrastructure already in place—largely State Route 4. Six Route 66 road segments in Illinois are listed in the National Register of Historic Places.

One small stretch in Auburn still features 1.4 miles of red-brick road laid over Portland cement, giving drivers a small glimpse into the conditions that drivers once faced. Driving along this patch of the Mother Road, it's easy to believe you've traveled back in time to 1931, when this red-brick carpet was laid out to welcome road travelers from near and far.

The Auburn Brick Road is located on Snell and Curran Roads, between Chatham and Auburn, Illinois. Head south from Chatham on Highway 4, and take a left on Snell Road (Historic US Route 66). Snell Road curves south and becomes Curran Road then rejoins Highway 4. Stop for a soda at Becky's Barn (5029 Snell Rd.), a small antiques shop located along the picture-perfect red-brick road.

Snell Road and Curran Road, Auburn, IL

LAND OF LINCOLN 📷

ABRAHAM LINCOLN'S HOME

In 1837, a young lawyer named Abraham Lincoln moved to Springfield, Illinois, the small town that eventually, thanks to his efforts, became the state capital. It was here that he became a successful lawyer, married Mary Todd in 1842, and delighted in the birth of his children. Springfield served as Lincoln's launching pad into the election of 1860.

Lincoln left an indelible mark on Springfield, and reminders of his incredible journey from humble state legislator to the pivotal 16th president of the United States are found all around town.

Courtesy of Illinois Office of Tourism

In 1844, Abraham Lincoln and his wife, Mary Todd Lincoln, moved into their first home, a small yet stately Greek Revival house located in downtown Springfield (8th and Jackson Streets) where they would live for 17 years. Mary's niece wrote of the home, "The little home was painted white and had green shutters. It was sweet and fresh, and Mary loved it. She was exquisitely dainty, and her house reflected her standards, with everything in good taste and in perfect order." Later, as their growing family made more space a necessity—three of their four sons were born here—the couple added a second floor, bringing the total number of rooms to twelve. The home has been beautifully, and accurately, restored to its original appearance and is now managed by the National Park Service. Note the stroll-worthy wood plank sidewalks that Lincoln would have walked upon on his way to the Old Illinois State Capitol Building, where he served as a state legislator. In the stately parlor, Lincoln received a delegation of party officials after winning the 1860 presidential nomination.

Abraham Lincoln's Home, 413 S. 8th St., Springfield, IL; (217) 492-4241; nps.gov/liho/index.htm

LINCOLN-HERNDON LAW OFFICES

Just opposite the Old State Capitol Building, the Lincoln-Herndon Law Offices (6th and Adams Streets), where Lincoln had an office from 1843 to about 1852, showcase Lincoln's early legal career. William H. Herndon, Lincoln's junior partner, once described his coworker's office habits: "When he reached the office, about nine o'clock in the morning, the first thing he did was to pick up a newspaper, spread himself out on an old sofa, one leg on a chair, and read aloud, much to my discomfort. Singularly enough Lincoln never read any other way but aloud. . . . Lincoln had always on the top of our desk a bundle of papers into which he slipped anything he wished to keep and afterwards refer to. It was a receptacle of general information. Some years ago, on removing the furniture from the office, I took down the bundle and blew from the top the liberal coat of dust that had accumulated thereon. Immediately underneath the string was a slip bearing this endorsement, in his hand: 'When you can't find it anywhere else, look in this.'"

The Greek Revival–style building's first floor still hosts an 1840s post office facility, just as it did when Lincoln worked here; Lincoln's actual office, which maintains its minimalist appearance marred only by the chaos of legal documents, is one of three located on the third floor.

Lincoln-Herndon Law Offices, 112 N. 6th St.; Springfield, IL; (217) 785-7289; abrahamlincolnonline.org/lincoln/sites/law.htm

LINCOLN DEPOT

Lincoln bade farewell to Springfield on Monday, February 11, 1861, from the Great Western Railroad Station, now known as the Lincoln Depot, located at 10th and Monroe Streets. From aboard his special inaugural train, the president-elect gave his eloquent Farewell Address to the thousands who had gathered to witness his departure and wish him well.

> My friends, no one, not in my situation, can appreciate my feeling of sadness at this parting. To this place and the kindness of these people, I owe everything. Here I have lived a quarter of a century, and have passed from a young to an old man. Here my children have been born, and one is buried. I now leave, not knowing when, or whether ever, I may return, with a task before me greater than that which rested upon Washington. Without the assistance of that Divine Being who ever attended him, I cannot succeed. With that assistance, I cannot fail. Trusting in Him who can go with me, and remain with you, and be everywhere for good, let us confidently hope that all will yet be well. To His care commending you, as I hope in your prayers you will commend me, I bid you an affectionate farewell.
>
> **–Abraham Lincoln, Farewell Address, February 11, 1861**

The sculptor of Lincoln's bust, Thomas Jones, remarked of the foreboding day and fond farewell: "It was a dark, gloomy, misty morning, boding rain. The people assembled early to say their last good-bye to the man they loved so much. The railroad office was used as the reception room. Lincoln took a position where his friends and neighbors could file by him in a line. As they came up each one took his hand in silence. The tearful eye, the tremulous lips, and inaudible words was a scene never to be forgotten. When the crowd has passed him, I stepped up to say good-bye. He gave me both his hands—no words after that. The train thundered in that was to bear him away, and Lincoln mounted the rear platform of one of the cars. Just at that moment Mrs. Lincoln's carriage drove up—it was raining. I proffered my umbrella and arm, and we approached Lincoln as near as we could for the crowd, and heard the last and best speech ever delivered in Springfield."

Today the Lincoln Depot is owned by a private law firm; however, the lower level remains open to visitors.

Lincoln Depot, 930 E. Monroe St., Springfield, IL; (217) 544-8695; lincolndepot.org

LINCOLN TOMB

Lincoln's 117-foot-tall granite tomb lies a few miles north of downtown Springfield in the historic Oak Ridge Cemetery (1500 Monument Ave.). His body had traveled nearly 1,700 miles from Washington, DC, in a special railroad car, before his official burial on May 4, 1865. Lincoln rests beside his wife and his sons Edward, William, and Thomas (Tad). Note the poignant tribute by Secretary of War Edwin Stanton, inscribed on the circular hallway leading to the burial chamber: "Now he belongs to the ages." Every Tuesday at 7 p.m., from June through August, volunteers in Civil War uniforms conduct a flag-lowering ceremony here, in tribute to one of the best leaders our nation has ever known.

The bronze bust of Lincoln might look familiar: It was designed by Gutzon Borglum, who also sculpted the face of Lincoln on Mount Rushmore. Visitors have rubbed the nose of Lincoln's bust here for decades, so much so that it seems to be polished in gold.

Lincoln Tomb, 1500 Monument Ave., Springfield, IL; lincolntomb.org

SPRINGFIELD'S ICONIC DINERS 📷

MAID-RITE DRIVE-THRU

In the early 1920s, an Iowa butcher named Fred Angell created a sandwich to remember. Using his butcher know-how, he combined the perfect cut of beef and ran it through his well-worn meat grinder. He then added a secret blend of spices, panfried it to perfection, and served it up on a steamed bun topped with mustard, pickles, and onions.

When a deliveryman tasted Fred's flavorful, deconstructed hamburger, he declared, "This sandwich is made right!," and the Maid-Rite sandwich was born.

Angell decided to sell the rights to his mouthwatering idea and ended up creating one of the very first food franchises in the US. Starting with his first location in his hometown of Muscatine, Iowa, Maid-Rite sandwich shops popped up across the Midwest. The tugboat-shaped Springfield Maid-Rite opened in 1924 and boasts the first-ever drive-thru in the US. Almost 100 years later, a Maid-Rite sandwich remains a Route 66 rite of passage.

THE MAID-RITE SANDWICH

Bite into a delightful, deconstructed hamburger at America's first drive-thru diner.

Little has changed at the red-and-white candy-striped shop. Maid-Rite sandwiches are still made fresh, from scratch, using Angeli's original recipe, and rolled up in wax paper. The root beer here is house-made, too; over 20 gallons are poured each day. Though you can pull up to the original drive-thru—once a walk-up window—it's worth dining inside, where small, wooden, schoolhouse-style tables are an unofficial tribute to the countless Springfield High School students who have called the Maid-Rite their home away from home over the years (the shop is located just a few blocks from the historic high school).

Maid-Rite, 118 N. Pasfield St., Springfield, IL; (217) 523-0723; maid-rite.com

COZY DOG DRIVE IN

A bit further down the Mother Road from the Maid-Rite, another historic diner beckons road travelers with the promise of belly-busting delights. To bite into a delectable corn dog at the Cozy Dog Drive In is to bite into history. That's because this ever-popular diner claims to have invented the cornbread-wrapped, deep-fried dog.

In 1959, Route 66 legend Bob Waldmire, an eighth grader at the time, interviewed his dad, Ed Waldmire Jr., owner of the Cozy Dog Drive In:

In Muskogee, Oklahoma, I saw an unusual sandwich called "corn-dog." This sandwich was a wiener baked in cornbread. The corn-dog was very good but took too long to prepare. The problem was how to cover a hotdog with batter and cook it in a short time.

In the fall of 1941, I told this story to a fellow student at Knox College whose father was in the bakery business and then gave it no further thought.

Five years later while in the Air Force stationed at Amarillo Airfield, I received a letter from my fellow student, Don Strand. To my surprise, he had developed a mix that would stick on a wiener while being french-fried. He wondered if he could send some down that I could try in Amarillo. Having plenty of spare time, I said "yes."

Using cocktail forks for sticks, the USO kitchen in which to experiment, we made a very tasty hotdog on a stick, that we called a "crusty cur." They became very popular both at the USO in town, and at the PX on the airfield. My friend continued to send mix, and we continued to sell thousands of crusty curs until I was discharged—honorably—in the spring of 1946.

We decided to sell them that spring. My wife did not like the name "crusty curs." Through trial and error and discarding dozens of names, we finally decided on the name "Cozy Dogs."

Cozy Dogs were officially launched at the Lake Springfield Beach House on June 16, 1946.

From the beach house, the Cozy Dogs made their way to the Illinois State Fair. They met such success that by 1949, Waldmire opened the brick-and-mortar Cozy Dog Drive In. The business remains in the Waldmire family to this day. Virginia Waldmire, Ed's wife, created the darling logo of two hugging hot dogs.

Cozy Dog Drive In, 2935 S. 6th St., Springfield, IL; (217) 525-1992; cozydogdrivein .com

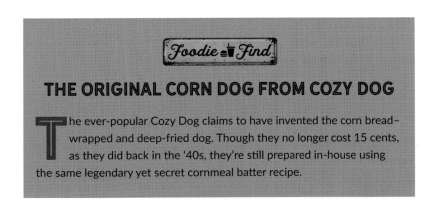

Foodie Find

THE ORIGINAL CORN DOG FROM COZY DOG

The ever-popular Cozy Dog claims to have invented the corn bread–wrapped and deep-fried dog. Though they no longer cost 15 cents, as they did back in the '40s, they're still prepared in-house using the same legendary yet secret cornmeal batter recipe.

DOC'S SODA FOUNTAIN

Once upon a time, secrets were shared, first loves blossomed, and friendships bloomed over fizzy sweet sodas. Behind the cold marble countertop, a soda "jerk" with a black bow tie and paper cap worked his magic, transforming flavored syrups and freshly carbonated water into drug store delights such as phosphates—tangy soda treats—floats, and egg creams. Swivel stool seating made it easy to enjoy a laugh with the friends flanking your sides. Sharing one soda with two straws was a sure sign of true love. Doc's Soda Fountain is a living souvenir of the 1920s, when the soda fountain was king.

Carbonated water was an early American health craze. Europeans, who long believed that effervescent mineral waters cured diseases, started the trend, inventing the first carbonating machines. Pharmacies initially offered soda water as a health tonic; they soon realized that the addition of sugary, flavored syrups increased business tenfold. At first the druggists themselves would serve up the soda concoctions, but later they left the job to dedicated soda jerks, named after the way they sharply tugged at the soda draft arm. By the 1920s, just about every apothecary featured a soda fountain.

Doc's, too, started out as a pharmacy only—Deck's Drug Store—in 1884. The soda fountain was added in 1929. At a time when Prohibition ruled out bars, the small-town apothecary's in-house soda shop became a go-to gathering spot.

Doc himself was a teacher in a one-room schoolhouse when he purchased the business, which is today run by his grandsons.

The pharmacy no longer operates within Doc's, but a small, in-house display features original items from Deck's 19th-century drug store, including everything a druggist needed to provide his patients with the ultimate in modern medicine, such as cocaine-laced syrups and even arsenic. In addition to soda treats prepared the old-fashioned way, Doc's Soda Fountain offers lunch, dinner, pies, and ice cream. Though the banana splits here are to die for, the hand-mixed phosphates offer a taste of the 1920s, before mass-bottled sodas swept onto the scene.

Soda fountains began disappearing in the 1970s thanks to the introduction of bottled soft drinks and self-serve soft drink dispensers, but Doc's endures as an ever-popular fixture of Girard, Illinois's, classic Midwestern main street.

133 S. 2nd St., Girard, IL; (217) 627-3491; facebook.com/DocsSodaFountain

Foodie Find

CHOCOLATE PHOSPHATE FROM DOC'S SODA FOUNTAIN

Sip an old-fashioned soda phosphate prepared by a tried-and-true jerk at this classic 1920s soda fountain.

SKY VIEW DRIVE-IN

Seeing a movie under the stars was a dazzling new experience in 1950 when the Sky View Drive-In opened for business. In the early years, cars packed the whopping 400 parking spots to catch the nightly double feature. At a time when many rural homes didn't have a black-and-white television, it gave families from the small town of Litchfield and its surrounding farms a place to spend some together time while also catching up with the most brilliant stars found near the end point of Route 66—Hollywood. Even babies were welcome to join in on the fun, as long as you promised to roll up the car windows if they began to cry.

Drive-ins also gave teenage couples a moment of escape. As soon as dusk set in, the make-out sessions began, hence their slick nickname: "passion pits."

In the 1950s, the Sky View was one of many drive-ins located along Route 66. Today it's the only originally operating drive-in on the Mother Road.

You can still catch a movie at the Sky View Drive-In, and perhaps even spot a falling star. The cinematic season runs from approximately early April until the end of October, rain or shine, only closing if the power goes out.

Drive-ins remain budget friendly. You're welcome to stay parked for a second screening. A full snack bar sells classic movie treats, including ice cream, candy, and popcorn, but you can also bring your own. Tickets are just $5 per person, and kids five and under are free.

In its early days, patrons were given small speakers that they could hang from their rolled-down car windows. Currently the movie soundtrack is available on 103.1 FM, a dedicated FM radio channel.

As always, the show starts at dusk.

1500 Old Route 66, Litchfield, IL; (217) 324-4451; litchfieldskyview.com

ARISTON CAFÉ

As the longest-operating restaurant along the entire stretch of US Route 66, the Ariston Café has seen countless travelers come and go since it opened all the way back in 1924.

It all started with Pete Adam, a young man who immigrated to the small town of Litchfield from Greece, in 1905. At first, Adam found success with a small candymaking business in nearby Carlinville. But his luck changed one day when a local doctor declared that the area was in desperate need of a good diner and instantly lent his patient, Adam, $1,000. Adam's son, Pete, recalled in a 2014 interview, "I asked my father, I said, 'What'd you do?' Dad said, 'Well. I got in my car, drove to St. Louis to find a cook.'"

Just as the doctor ordered, Adam founded the now-iconic Ariston Café in Carlinville, on the original alignment of the Mother Road, later relocating along with the route to Litchfield in 1935, a few years after yet another realignment. The twin gas pumps that once greeted drivers were removed long ago; otherwise little has changed since the day Adam first realized his American dream. The exterior is utilitarian, with nods to the Art Deco style popular during its construction visible in the half-moon-topped front façade and glazed terra-cotta coping; inside, people have been hunkering down over steaming cups of coffee at the same old-school diner countertop with its chrome swivel stools, or snuggling up at the handcrafted wooden booths, for decades.

The Ariston's motto, "Remember Where Good Food Is Served," is reflected in the endless menu. Dishes are listed from across the US, from hand-cut Texas steaks to Southern-style fried chicken to Southwest favorites such as enchiladas, burritos, and tacos. Greek favorites, once considered exotic fare in small-town Litchfield,

Courtesy of Illinois Office of Tourism

include Athenian-style salad, gyro sandwiches, and chicken livers seasoned with lemon and oregano. Old-school menu items—think liver and onions, grilled chicken livers, pork chops, ham steaks, and open-faced steak sandwiches with gravy—remain ever-popular at the Ariston. Friday and Saturday nights boast prime rib; the Sunday buffet, with its omelet and hand-carved roast beef stations, packs the house.

The legendary homemade desserts are not to be missed. Peanut butter cup pie and cherry-topped cheesecake are among the most popular, but it's the traditional, fresh baklava that makes regulars' mouths water when they spot the neon Ariston sign in the distance.

Budweiser remains the beer of choice, though it no longer costs just 15 cents a pint as it did when the restaurant first opened its doors.

413 Old Route 66 N., Litchfield, IL; (217) 324-2023; ariston-cafe.com

HENRY'S RABBIT RANCH 📷

Rabbit Rancher Rich Henry is an expert in wrangling both the cotton-tailed critters and the Volkswagen-created automobile species. You can't miss this quirky, sprawling ranch, which fronts the 1930–40 alignment of Route 66; nor can you miss falling in love with the furry friends that live here.

In the early 1990s, Henry traveled the length of Route 66. Along the way, he noted a dearth of visitor centers along the Mother Road. Back

Courtesy of Illinois Office of Tourism

home in the small coal-mining town of Staunton, he decided to transform his ranch into a one-of-a-kind tourist destination dedicated to the historic byway. Over the years, he gathered old Route 66 highway and trucking memorabilia, including a replica of a 1940s era gas station (which houses the actual visitor's center and souvenir shop) and a half-dozen junked VW Rabbits, which he buried, rear fenders facing the sky.

But the bunnies that call this corner of Route 66 home are the real draw. It all started when Rich's daughter received a pair of rabbits as a gift. Before long, their loving instincts led to babies upon babies—too many babies to squeeze into a single-room apartment. Dad stepped in to save the day, offering to raise the cuddly grandbabies on his ranch. Over the years, injured rabbits, brought to the ranch by locals, added to the ranch's burgeoning bunny population. Each bunny holds a special name and sports a unique personality. The ranch serves as a sanctuary, so rest assured that the cute bunny you're petting isn't going to end up on anyone's dinner plate. The rabbits roam the grassy ranch land, unless it's too cold outside, when they graze the souvenir shop.

The bunnies are buried beneath tiny headstones bearing their names in a dedicated cemetery. The poignant Tomb of the Unknown Bunny pays tribute to the many wild rabbits that have tragically fallen victim to speeding cars along Route 66.

1107 Old Route 66, Staunton, IL; (618) 635-5655; henrysroute66.com

WORLD'S LARGEST CATSUP BOTTLE ◉

It rises, majestically, from the prairie landscape, a beacon of hope for condiment-crazy motorists. The 70-foot-high World's Largest Catsup Bottle, beloved by the all the french fry and burger lovers making their way along Route 66, has made mouths water since it was erected atop 100-foot steel legs back in 1949.

Once upon a time, motorists driving through Collinsville, Illinois, were greeted with the sweet smell of catsup. Back in 1891, a group of local businessmen raised $5,000 to create their common fortune: the Collinsville Canning and Packing Company. The catsup factory found great success thanks to its secret, tangy recipe. The operation survived the Great Depression, reaching number-one catsup status in the US.

When the booming factory needed a water tower, they created one that doubled as an advertisement. Despite local legends, the bottle-shaped tower holds 100,000 gallons of water and not catsup.

When bottling operations were moved to Indiana in the early 1960s, the old factory became a warehouse, and the sharp smell of catsup ceased wafting through town.

Thankfully, local preservationists fought to keep the World's Largest Catsup Bottle standing.

The best time to roll into Collinsville is in July, when the World's Largest Catsup Bottle Festival celebrates the oversize bottle's birthday with a Little Princess Tomato and Sir Catsup Contest, a catsup taste test, smothered-in-catsup tater tot and hot dog eating contests, music, and more. Want to give Collinsville's catsup a try? It's still available online, by the bottle or case.

800 S. Morrison Ave., Collinsville, IL; catsupbottle.com

CAHOKIA MOUNDS STATE HISTORIC SITE 👟

Once upon a time, one of the greatest cities of the world—Cahokia—rose like the sun on the horizon of the Midwestern prairie. Larger than London, its population reached around 20,000 at its peak, between 1050 and 1150, and stretched over six square miles. Built by the native Mississippians, this sophisticated and prosperous capital served as the agricultural, cultural, religious, and economic center of the Mississippi River Valley.

The Mississippians used astronomical alignments to plan what was at the time a busy metropolis. Using woven baskets to transport the earth, they built 120 earthen mounds with a 100-foot-tall mega mound, a place of worship and ceremony, at the city's center. The Mississippians lived in rectangle-shaped homes with thatched roofs, all connected by courtyards and streets, in the surrounding hamlets.

Yet by 1350, this stately city lay abandoned—and no one knows exactly why. The harsh winters, wind, and river flooding threatened to wipe it off the map completely. It wasn't until the 18th century that the land was resettled, this time by French missionaries, and it took a local dentist, who surveyed the site in the late 1880s, to understand its historic significance.

Today, the remnants of Cahokia, the most sophisticated prehistoric native civilization north of Mexico, are carefully preserved at Cahokia Mounds State Historic Site, located just a few miles off of Route 66, west of Collinsville, Illinois.

Of the original earthen mounds, 68 are preserved. The most remarkable is Monks Mound, which once dominated the prairie as the largest prehistoric earthen structure in the New World. At 100 feet tall, 955 feet long, and 775 feet wide, with four terraces, the soil- and clay-formed mound was as big as the Great Pyramid of Giza. Climb to the top—an easy 154 steps—and you'll be met with a view of nearby St. Louis in the distance.

Just west of Monks Mound lies a reconstruction of the Midwestern version of Stonehenge. This unique sun calendar, created with a series of evenly spaced wooden posts, is known as Woodhenge. To this day, locals and history buffs gather at Woodhenge on the solar equinox and solstice, to watch the sun line up with the wooden posts.

Public tours are offered April through November, but you can also rent an iPod, available in the Museum Shop, that will guide you, via an interactive app, along three outdoor trails.

Archaeologists remain puzzled by Cahokia's fate. No clear evidence exists indicating that war or disease wreaked havoc here, leading some to believe that the city was abandoned due to social unrest or perhaps climate change. Did flooding force its inhabitants out? Drought? Deforestation? The Mississippians left no written records, however, and the once-sacred site, so important to its people that it was built to align with the sun, moon, and stars, remains a mystery.

30 Ramey St., Collinsville, IL; (618) 346-5160; cahokiamounds.org

LUNA CAFÉ 🎞️

In the dark of the night, long before LED lit up America's roadways, Luna Café's seven-color neon sign, featuring a swanky martini glass and promising steaks, chicken, and seafood, was a welcome beacon of light in the distance. Pulling up to the café, a neon half-moon smiles cheekily from above the front entrance. Yet this seemingly quaint, small-town roadhouse had more on its menu than good grub. Regular, randy Route 66 drivers knew that if the sweet red maraschino cherry in the martini glass was aglow, girls were ready and waiting in the undercover upstairs brothel.

Downstairs, a gambling operation tempted travelers with the hope of doubling or even tripling their funds, though no doubt in the end, most left the Luna Café, Route

66's den of illegal delights, empty-pocketed. Good old mobster Al Capone at times operated here, using it as a safe house as he ran his many bootleg operations.

Luna Café opened in 1924, and though its gambling den and upstairs of ill-repute are long gone, its lovingly restored neon signs are among the oldest along the route. In its early years, the Luna Café was not a simple roadhouse but an expensive "fine dining establishment" that few locals could afford; now, on any given Friday or Saturday night, it's packed with locals.

No matter the restrictions of today, Luna Café remains a rollicking roadside stop. Play an old tune on the jukebox, saddle up at the bar, and meet the locals, or give the slot machines a gamble. See if you can spot your state from the thousands of old license plates that cover the walls.

201 E. Chain of Rocks Rd., Granite City, IL; (618) 931-3152

CHAIN OF ROCKS BRIDGE 📷

Route 66 travelers once crossed the mighty Mississippi atop the Old Chain of Rocks Bridge, a 5,353-foot-long link between Illinois and Missouri. Named after the force behind the rocky rapids—a 17-mile-long shoal that once made this stretch of the Mississippi extremely dangerous to navigate—a 22-degree bend in the middle allowed for the safe passage of the riverboats that still relied on the river at the time construction began, on both sides of the river, in 1927.

When the bridge first started welcoming traffic in 1929, it was considered a marvel of engineering. Five trusses forming ten spans are perched 55 feet above the river. It cost $2.5 million to build, a stratospheric amount at the time.

In 1936, the river became a part of Route 66, shortening the distance between Edwardsville, Illinois, and St. Louis, Missouri, by 15 miles, a boon to drivers.

Courtesy of Missouri Division of Tourism

But by the early 1960s, Route 66 had been rerouted, and the bridge was in dire need of repair, having become too narrow at 24 feet wide to accommodate modern vehicles and too dilapidated to even allow for the safe passage of older ones. In 1966, a bigger bridge—the Interstate 270 Bridge—opened just 2,000 feet upstream, and the old bridge, closed off to the public, sadly awaited its demolition fate.

Thankfully, in the 1980s, a group called Trailnet saw its potential as a historic pedestrian passageway and began to push for restoration. In 1999, the Old Chain of Rocks Bridge reopened to hikers and bikers as part of the Route 66 Bikeway in 1999.

Today you'll have to cross by bike or foot, but it's easy to imagine what it would have been like riding across this beauty of a bridge in the early years of Route 66. Little has been altered over the years, except for a disguise coating of green paint that covered bright red segments during World War I. The vistas of the Mississippi River and its scenic banks, with the Gateway Arch in the distance, as well as the amazing architecture of the bridge itself, are best captured at today's slower pace.

Chain of Rocks Road (Granite City, IL) and St. Louis Riverfront Trail at Riverview Drive (St. Louis, MO)

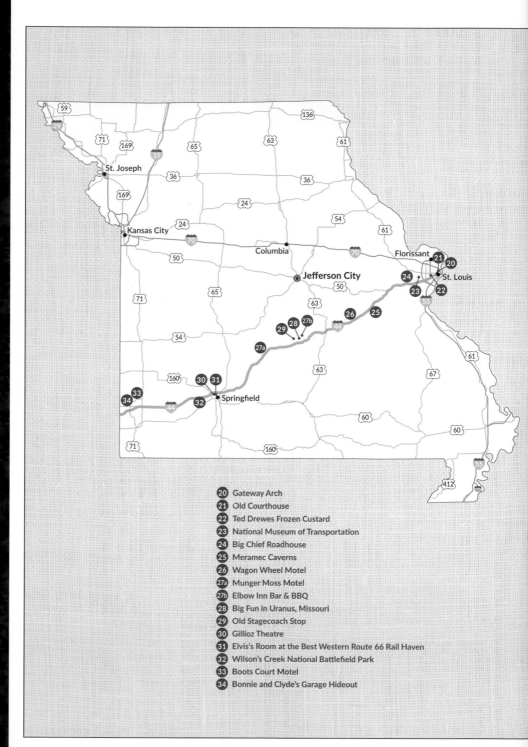

20 Gateway Arch
21 Old Courthouse
22 Ted Drewes Frozen Custard
23 National Museum of Transportation
24 Big Chief Roadhouse
25 Meramec Caverns
26 Wagon Wheel Motel
27a Munger Moss Motel
27b Elbow Inn Bar & BBQ
28 Big Fun in Uranus, Missouri
29 Old Stagecoach Stop
30 Gillioz Theatre
31 Elvis's Room at the Best Western Route 66 Rail Haven
32 Wilson's Creek National Battlefield Park
33 Boots Court Motel
34 Bonnie and Clyde's Garage Hideout

GATEWAY ARCH 📷 👟

It's our nation's tallest monument, 900 tons of gleaming stainless steel reaching 630 feet into the sky above the western bank of the Mississippi River, from the very spot where St. Louis was founded. This poignant symbol recognizes the many pioneers who risked everything to cross the Mississippi toward new lives, linking not just east and west but, as noted by Vice President Hubert Humphrey on the day of its dedication, May 25, 1965, "the rich heritage of yesterday with the richer future of tomorrow."

It's fitting that St. Louis was chosen as the site of this tribute to Thomas Jefferson's role in westward expansion, most notably his commission of the Corps of Discovery Expedition (1804–06), led by Meriwether Lewis and William Clark, to explore the territory acquired in the Louisiana Purchase. Lewis and Clark launched their voyage of discovery into the vast, wild western wilderness from St. Louis.

Though the feasibility of creating such an overreaching arch was questioned, Finnish-American industrial planner Eero Saarinen won the design competition in 1948, beating out his very own father, who had proposed a tall rectangular stone gate. The total cost: $13 million, a massive amount at the time.

The Gateway Arch stands, above all, as a marvel of modern structural design. It took powerful cranes, derricks, and an incredible amount of manpower to raise and connect each of the 142 triangular sections, which narrow as they soar toward the stars. Each leg of the arch was so precisely linked that if either had been off by even 1/64th of an inch, they wouldn't have met in the middle, a prospect that many at the time believed would be the final disastrous result.

In late October 1965, construction crews prepared to literally connect east and west as the monument stood ready to be locked into place with the final keystone. Firefighters were called in to cool the steel with cold water since early fall temperatures were causing it to expand. A Catholic priest and a rabbi prayed over the keystone as it was precariously inserted. Finally, the last section slid into place, and St. Louis breathed a giant sigh of relief.

Though its construction was daunting, the elegant monument can withstand high winds—it's designed to sway up to 18 inches—and even an earthquake.

Weighing a whopping 17,246 tons, the flattened catenary arch hides a tram system that whisks visitors to the observation deck at the arch's apex, where, on a clear day, you can see about 30 miles into the distance. For the claustrophobic, the four-minute ride to the top in the tiny tramcar can be a nail-biter, but it offers an unparalleled look into the incredible inner mechanics of the monument. The prize for surviving the journey to the top: 16 windows on each side that offer impressive views of St. Louis and the Mississippi River as well as a seemingly endless glimpse into the journey ahead along the rambling westbound Route 66.

St. Louis, MO; (877) 982-1410; gatewayarch.com

OLD COURTHOUSE 📷

Standing on the steps of the east entrance of St. Louis's Old Courthouse, it's difficult to imagine the hard reality that less than 160 years ago men and women were auctioned off as slaves, here, to the highest bidder.

St. Louis had always served as a major market in slavery, with deep Southerners traveling upstream to bid on slaves to supply free farm labor, and St. Louis was long known for its slave patrols, officers who searched for runaways. When a slave's owner died, either without a will or having gone bankrupt, they were sold on these very steps, which once served as a public slave auction block. An estimated 533 slaves were offered for sale here on the steps of this "temple of justice." The last slave auction held at the Old Courthouse took place in 1861.

In 1846, two slaves, Dred and Harriet Scott, bravely and defiantly sued for their freedom in this hallowed courthouse. The case made its way to the Supreme Court, where the 1857 Dred Scott Decision ruled that slaves and their descendants were

not protected by the US Constitution, a verdict that, though terribly unjust, ultimately helped rally support for President Abraham Lincoln's Emancipation Proclamation.

The Scotts weren't the only ones to alter the course of our nation from this history-filled courthouse. Women's suffrage activist Virginia Minor was also tried here in 1873, whereupon she argued that the Fourteenth Amendment gave women the right to vote. The Supreme Court of Missouri ruled against Minor, and though she appealed to the Supreme Court of the United States, they too agreed with the Missouri court's decision. Nevertheless, the verdict spurred the suffragists to keep on fighting for their right to vote.

Construction of the courthouse began in 1828, but over the decades it has experienced countless renovations. The iconic Italian Renaissance cast-iron dome, modeled on St. Peter's Basilica in Vatican City, was installed between 1860–64. Note the murals on the four lunettes, eye-shape openings visible on the interior of the dome, which depict four key events in St. Louis history: the 1780 British-Indian attack on St. Louis; Pierre Laclède selecting the site of St. Louis in 1763; DeSoto discovering the Mississippi River in 1541; and the Cochetopa Pass in the Colorado Rockies, an unsuccessful attempt, financed by a group of St. Louis businessmen in 1848, to find a route over Cochetopa Pass for the first transcontinental railroad.

By 1930, St. Louis had outgrown the Old Courthouse, and the new Civil Courts Building was built just a few blocks to the west.

Today the old courthouse serves as a powerful place of memory. Several restored courtrooms, educational dioramas, and galleries take visitors back in time to the days when it was the setting for legal battles that changed the course of US history.

11 N. 4th St., St. Louis, MO; (877) 982-1410; gatewayarch.com/experience/old-courthouse.aspx

TED DREWES FROZEN CUSTARD 🍦

You could say that Ted Drewes is in the memory-making business.

That's because for decades this wooden icicle–trimmed palace has been serving families two very merry delights: creamy, indulgent, old-fashioned frozen custard and . . . Christmas trees!

Ted Drewes's story begins way back in the roaring twenties, in the warmer climes of Florida. Drewes was a legendary tennis player . . . long before tennis was considered a professional sport. During the summertime he operated a swimming pool in St. Louis; winters were spent in Florida, where he both played and taught tennis. Ever the

TED DREWES'S CONCRETE

I n 1959, the concrete—frozen custard with your choice of a mix-in addition blended into a treat so thick and creamy that it can be served upside-down—was added to the menu at the iconic icicle-trimmed palace that is Ted Drewes.

entrepreneur, he began selling frozen custard, ice cream's rich cousin, on the carnival circuit to supplement his income, eventually opening his first custard stand in Florida in 1929.

Drewes met so much success that by 1941 he had opened three additional Ted Drewes Frozen Custard shops in St. Louis. His winning motto: "Our Business Is Service." Summertime soon became synonymous with at least once-weekly trips to Ted Drewes, while a pit stop for a custard or a concrete at the Chippewa Street location quickly became a Route 66 rite of passage.

Then came the usual winter slow season. Drewes would not be daunted. He came up with yet another brilliant idea. Christmas trees! During the cold months, you'll find spruces, pines, and firs lining the parking lot. Hot cocoa replaces cold custard. Drewes Christmas tree business boomed, so much so that he even invested in a Christmas tree farm in Nova Scotia, the balsam fir capital of the world.

Little has changed over the years. The frozen custard recipe, which is packed with butterfat enriched with egg yolks, is the same one used since the 1920s. The business remains in the Drewes family, with Ted Senior's grandkids now running the show.

6726 Chippewa St., St. Louis, MO; (314) 481-2652; teddrewes.com

NATIONAL MUSEUM OF TRANSPORTATION 📷

Calling all gearheads!

At the National Museum of Transportation, all the cars that once traveled along Route 66, from the early days to today, are polished and ready to hit the pavement. This 42-acre car culture mecca is dedicated to the restoration and preservation of our nation's transportation history.

Make a beeline to the Earl C. Lindberg Automobile Center, located within the museum, where, before the backdrop of a Route 66 mid-century drive-in, more than 200 rare vintage vehicles rest eternally in all their shiny chrome glory. You might feel as if you've stepped into an old-fashioned car dealership and you're right: Earl C. Lindberg was a St. Louis Cadillac dealer who also developed the car leasing concept in the US. Too bad that none of the beautiful Corvettes, Cadillacs, Model Ts, and Mustangs on display here are for sale.

The fascinating cars here range from a 1901 one-cylinder, seven-horsepower St. Louis Motor Carriage Co. automobile, which once cost $1,200 and is one of only nine still in existence, to a 1923 steam-powered Stanley Steamer, to a Chrysler turbine car, one of only 55 produced by Chrysler and considered incredibly high-tech when it hit the market in 1963.

The museum also houses one of the largest and best collections of rail transportation in North America, including the 1870s mule-driven streetcar named "Bellefontaine #33," which led to the founding of the private museum in 1944, when a group of preservation-minded citizens acquired the junkyard-bound streetcar but then realized they need a place to both restore and house it.

Courtesy of Missouri Division of Tourism

Other don't-miss rail-focused finds include a 1920s Pullman sleeping car; "Big Boy," the world's largest successful steam locomotive; and the Frisco #1621, a steam locomotive that was built in the US for czarist Russia but was never shipped because of the impending revolution. The museum even boasts its very own railway spur to an active main line, formerly owned by the Missouri Pacific Railroad, now by the Union Pacific Railroad, so larger pieces of railroad equipment can roll right to the museum. Children love riding the miniature railroad and the full-size restored trolley that remain in operation on the museum's grounds. In addition to trains and automobiles, you'll also find planes, buses, horse-drawn carriages, and even a tugboat.

Try to plan a visit around one of the many car shows hosted by the museum, when classic car lovers from local clubs gather to show off their treasured cars of days gone by.

2933 Barrett Station Rd., St. Louis, MO; (314) 965-6212; transportmuseumassocia tion.org

BIG CHIEF ROADHOUSE

In the early days of Route 66, roadhouses were a dime a dozen. After a long day on the road, you could always count on being greeted with music, dancing, sometimes gambling, and always a cold beer and belly-filling fare.

As travelers hit the route just west of St. Louis, they knew that the Big Chief Roadhouse, originally called the Big Chief Hotel, was ready to welcome them with full-service dining as well as a place to hang their hat for the night.

At two stories tall, the Spanish Mission Revival roadhouse, with its white stucco walls and terra-cotta rooftop, recalls Santa Fe—the city that lies about 1,000 miles to the west—more than St. Louis.

Big Chief opened for business in 1928 and has the pavement to thank for its early success: the segment of Route 66 that it fronts was one of the earliest to be paved. As one of the biggest and earliest cabin courts along the highway, it boasted 62 cabins, each

Liezl Moss

with its very own garage, hot and cold running shower baths, a full-service restaurant, a playground, a gas station, a grocery store, and even a Mission-style (false) bell tower that served as a roadside beacon of sorts. A 9,000-square-foot garden grew all the fresh veggies and fruits served on the premises. In the evening, staff pushed aside the dining room tables of the restaurant and the rollicking dancing began. The cost of a night's stay? Just $1.50.

Though sadly the bell tower and cabins were demolished in the years after Route 66 was rerouted in 1932, the full-service restaurant not only survived but thrives. Happy hour—Monday through Friday 4 to 6 p.m. and Sunday from 11 a.m. to 6 p.m.—is the happiest time to visit thanks to great food and drink specials. Though the indulgent steak dinner no longer costs 75 cents, as it did during the roadhouse's earliest years, crowds still rush in on Tuesday for the $12 steak night special.

17352 Manchester Rd., Wildwood, MO; (636) 458-3200; bigchiefstl.com

MERAMEC CAVERNS

On December 7, 1869, a budding 22-year-old outlaw named Jesse James robbed the Daviess County Savings Association bank in Gallatin, Missouri, killing the cashier. The state's governor offered a whopping $5,000 reward for the capture of James, and for the next dozen years, until his death in 1882, he eluded capture, becoming America's most infamous bandit, sticking up not only banks but also stagecoaches and trains. Legend states that James once claimed Meramec Caverns, a complex of more than 6,000 surveyed limestone caves hidden beneath the rolling hills of the Meramec Valley, as his impenetrable hideout.

It took over 400 million years to form the underground wonder that is the Meramec Caverns. An underwater river carved the many chambers, while seeping water carried

Courtesy of Missouri Division of Tourism

calcite through cracks in the ceiling, forming the magnificent stalactites and stalagmites that festoon the floors and ceilings that make Meramec Caverns one of the most marvelous natural wonders along Route 66. It's also one of the most advertised attractions, as you've undoubtedly seen the many ads on billboards, barns, and buildings leading up to the spectacular sight.

Before Jesse James claimed the caves as his hideout, the native Osage Indians used them as a refuge from extreme weather conditions. In the early 1700s, French explorer Phillip Renault entered the caves, hoping to find gold, after his Osage guide mentioned that the walls were lined with glittering yellow metal. His hopes for finding a treasure trove of gold were dashed when he realized that the shimmery veins were instead saltpeter, a valuable find of another kind. Saltpeter was a key ingredient used in manufacturing gunpowder at that time, and Renault's inadvertent discovery launched close to 150 years of years of saltpeter mining that ended abruptly in 1864 when Confederate troops destroyed an in-cave Union gunpowder factory.

Among the many wonders you'll encounter on the 1.25-mile guided tour of this seven-level system, you'll find a 70-foot-tall rock formation that lives up to its nickname, "Stage Curtain." You won't find wine in the cave's Wine Room, but you will find a 6-foot-tall onyx table that's been naturally decorated by botryoids, deposit clusters that look strikingly like grapes. The cave even boasts a ballroom with a natural air-conditioning system that has been hosting dances since the late 1800s.

Local Lester Dill purchased the cave in the 1930s and put it on the map of Route 66 must-sees thanks to his ingenious invention: the bumper sticker. While tourists embarked on guided tours of Dills' caverns, "Bumper Sign Boys" tied wooden signs to their cars, making for a free souvenir . . . and free advertising for the cave tours. Later, self-adhesive stickers replaced placards, and the caves have been booming with visitors to today.

1135 Highway W., Sullivan, MO; (573) 468-2283; americascave.com

WAGON WHEEL MOTEL 🛏

The Wagon Wheel Motel, Café, and Station in Cuba, Missouri, has been serving travelers along Route 66 since 1936. Cozy cottages made of gorgeous Ozark stone still greet guests looking to rest for the night while an old-fashioned Standard Oil filling station recalls the early days of gas-guzzling road trips along the Mother Road. You'll know you've arrived when you spot the original neon sign with its red wagon wheel.

Built at a time when the nation was struggling to dig itself out of the Depression and Dust Bowl, the Wagon Wheel represented optimism and hope for a new era that allowed for the luxury of exploring the US by automobile.

The 1939 American Automobile Association directory listed the Wagon Wheel Motel as "one of the finest courts in the state," boasting nine stone cottages with private tubs or shower baths, gas heat, fans in the summertime, enclosed garages, and splendid surroundings—all luxuries for the era. A filling station serviced often unreliable automobiles; the Wagon Wheel Café filled hungry travelers with American diner favorites. The charming Tudor Revival cottages were built by a local stonemason, and the original owners, Margaret and Robert Martin, added more units over the years. Today 14 small cabins greet guests.

Courtesy of Missouri Division of Tourism

In September 2009, Connie Echols stepped in to save the Wagon Wheel, painstakingly restoring each of the individual motel cottages back to their original luster. The original wood doors with their glass knobs open to reveal quaint rooms with original hardwood floors and steam registers. If you're lucky, you might be able to check into Room 16, where a coin-operated "Magic Fingers" bed from the '60s still vibrates—bring your quarters.

In 2011, the Wagon Wheel Motel, the oldest continuously operating motel on US 66, celebrated its 75th anniversary. "There's nothing in the world like the Wagon Wheel," gushes Echols. "I meet the nicest people, from all around, all of them looking to capture the spirit of Route 66. Everyone is thrilled to check into a classic motel that has survived all these years on the Mother Road."

901 E. Washington St., Cuba, MO; (573) 885-3411; wagonwheel66cuba.com

MUNGER MOSS MOTEL AND THE ELBOW INN

The Munger Moss Motel's neon sign has been attracting road-roaming automobiles like moths to lamplight since the iconic cabin court opened in in 1946. Best known for its warm, family-style hospitality, the Munger Moss is a living legend in the Ozarks.

Munger Moss originally referred to a sandwich shop in Devils Elbow, Missouri, famous for its barbecue. Owners Nellie Munger and her husband, Emmitt Moss, combined their names to create the unique moniker, Munger Moss Sandwich Shop. When Route 66 was rerouted in 1942, to accommodate heavy military traffic going to and from nearby Fort Leonard Wood, the shop, together with its top-secret barbecue recipe, moved to Lebanon, Missouri.

And though many independent early motels were lost to time when Route 66 was eventually bypassed by Interstate 44, Munger-Moss held tight to its success. The motel's ingenious owner at the time planted a large painted sign on the newfangled highway, as well as a makeshift bridge that steered drivers toward the Munger Moss.

Today the Munger Moss Motel's glowing neon sign still shines bright, with a little help from the Neon Heritage Preservation Committee, the Route 66 Association of Missouri, and the National Park Service, all of which stepped in to help fund the restoration.

Foodie Find

DEVILS ELBOW BBQ PULLED PORK SANDWICH

The Munger Moss Sandwich Shop became such a popular roadside spot that by 1946 a new owner added a 14-room cabin court with car parking in the middle so barbecue connoisseurs could sleep off their barbeque pulled pork sandwiches on-site.

Forty-four rooms and 16 efficiencies welcome guests from all over the world. Owners Bob and Ramona Lehman have been operating the motel since the early 1970s, and the motel maintains its mom-and-pop motel status. "When Bob and I came here in 1971, rooms rented from $7.50 to $9.00. We still try to keep our rates reasonable," explains owner Ramona Lehman. "I love welcoming guests from around the world. I treat them as if they're the most important people in the world. I give most guests a hug when they leave. There's no place in the world quite like the Munger Moss Motel."

1336 Route 66, Lebanon, MO; (417) 532-3111; mungermoss.com

While you're in Lebanon, head over to Devils Elbow and pay a visit to the original sandwich shop, now named the Elbow Inn (21050 Teardrop Rd.). Built in 1936, it's still a famous stop for finger-licking barbecue sandwiches. Be sure to drive across the beautiful old steel-truss bridge that crosses the once-treacherous bend of the Big Piney River known as Devils Elbow: it dates to the early days of Route 66, and from it you can admire the 200-foot-tall bluffs of Gasconade dolomite, one of the seven scenic wonders of Missouri.

21050 Teardrop Rd., Devils Elbow, MO; (573) 336-5375

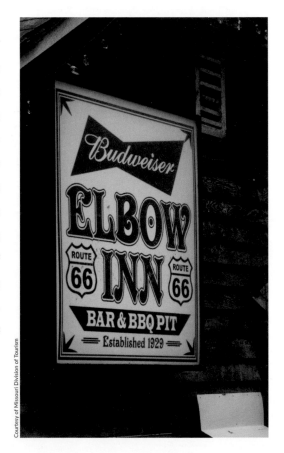

BIG FUN IN URANUS 📷 🗂️

If you've never explored Uranus . . . you're in for an adventure.

It's not a planet . . . it's a destination. This strip mall of a town, wrapped up in a Wild Western façade, is the home of all things kooky and wonderful.

Adventures abound in Uranus. Where else can you get a tattoo, compete in an axe-throwing contest, shoot a rifle, shop for fudge, catch a rollicking burlesque act, or . . . get married? Anything is possible in Uranus.

This stellar town popped up in 2000, when Louie Keen, owner of the in-town Big Louie's Burlesque Saloon, added a Chicken Bones Party Bar and Grill and Skin City Tattoo Studio to his ever-growing strip mall along the Mother Road. In 2016, he added a

Uranus Inc.

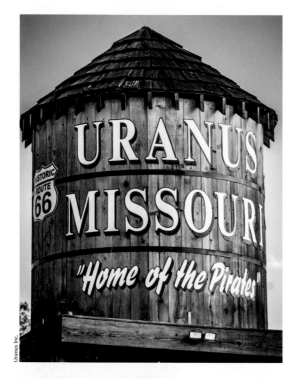

fudge factory, named the strip mall stretch of a town Uranus, and called it a day.

Though few people consider this corner of Route 66 home, thousands of visitors descend upon Uranus throughout the year. Keen considers himself the mayor of this wacky destination, which also lays claim to the world's largest belt buckle, as verified by the *Guinness Book of World Records*.

The vibe here is decidedly adult, thanks to the saloon, distillery, shotgun wedding chapel, ever-popular burlesque show, tattoo parlor, and gun range, but it somehow manages to be family-friendly at the same time as the Uranus humor often flies easily overhead. Kids love the climbable Uranus Fire Department engine, food trucks, and the fun-filled fudge shop, which offers 18 flavors a day as well as just about every gag gift available on the planet.

Be prepared to give in to the corny puns, which pop up everywhere on billboards leading up to the out-of-this-world destination.

"We are having big fun in Uranus."

"The best fudge is found in Uranus!"

"Uranus Brake Repair—Keeping skid marks out of Uranus."

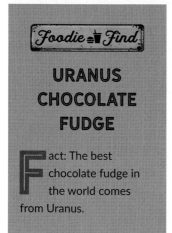

Foodie Find

URANUS CHOCOLATE FUDGE

Fact: The best chocolate fudge in the world comes from Uranus.

14400 Hwy. Z, St. Robert, MO; (573) 336-8758; uranusmissouri.com

OLD STAGECOACH STOP 🚌

Long before motorists began zooming across the US along Route 66, the treacherous trip west was made via stagecoach. These typically four-wheeled, closed carriages, drawn by four horses, made regular trips between stations, a.k.a. stages, where the coach's horses were replaced and passengers enjoyed a hot meal and lodging for the night. The Old Stagecoach Stop, a double-pen log cabin built in 1854, once serviced the coaches and travelers that rolled into town along the St. Louis to Springfield stage route. With each of its rooms restored to a different era, this small museum offers unique insight into its journey through time, from residence and tavern on the Western frontier of the

Wikimedia Commons

1850s to its final chapter as a boarding house for soldiers and their wives in the early 1960s.

The stop played a key role in the Civil War, as both supplies and men were transported along the stagecoach trail that stretched before the inn. Though initially the prevalent support in Pulaski County remained with the South, opinions shifted as the Civil War was imminent, leaving friends and families on opposite sides of the battlefield. The Union set up a fort on the hill above the town square, carefully guarding the road, which became known as Wire Road when telegraph wire was strung on poles the entire length. In 1862, the inn was transformed into a Union hospital.

Wire Road would become Route 66 in the early 1920s, and the stagecoach stop served as a hotel and boarding house for a new generation of westward travelers. When Mother Road traffic dwindled, so did business, and though it closed in the 1980s, today the Old Stagecoach Stop is restored and open again to share its history, which mirrors the development of Pulaski County. A guided tour of the 10 lovingly restored rooms, each representative of a different significant period in building's past, is led by a volunteer in period costume and takes about 45 minutes.

105 N. Lynn St., Waynesville, MO; (573) 336-3561; oldstagecoachstop.org

GILLIOZ THEATRE

On October 11, 1926, one month to the day before Route 66 officially opened for business, a crowd gathered in long lines stretching a block long from the box office of the magnificent Gillioz Theater, the gem of Springfield, Missouri. At 6 p.m., the doors swung open for an evening of dancing and a double feature. All the seats—595 on orchestra level and 420 in the balcony—were filled, and a worldly sense of glamour and excitement that the budding city of Springfield had never witnessed filled the air.

Contractor M. E. Gillioz was best known for building bridges. His bridges crossed rivers throughout the Route 66–linked states of Missouri, Oklahoma, and Kansas. He

GILLIOZ

ARTHUR'S STONE , MERLIN'S FIRE
APRIL 30 - MAY 2

GILLIOZ THEATRE
SATO 48 AWARDS
MAY 6 AT 7PM

built his beloved Gillioz Theatre out of the infrastructure construction materials he knew best—steel and concrete; you'll only find wood in the handrails, doors, and doorframes.

Gillioz spared no expense, either: The original cost of the Spanish Colonial Revival building with its terra-cotta tiling was $300,000, a large sum at the time. The interior was altogether sumptuous, as noted by the town newspaper, the *Springfield Leader*: "Beautifully tinted walls, exquisite tapestries and elaborate pillars, with a blue and gold color scheme, make up the main entrance. Overlooking the main lobby is the promenade which is also elaborately decorated along the same lines as that of the lobby. The lobby, promenade and foyer will be handsomely appointed in expensively designed furniture, carrying out the general scheme of decorations." Nicknamed "Theatre Beautiful," the Gillioz was a premier stopping point along Route 66, popular with both locals and out-of-towners. Even Elvis and Ronald Reagan caught a show in the famous theater. Recently restored, the lobby and auditorium remain much the same as they did on opening day, making every show at the Gillioz a historic, embracing experience for both the theater patron and performer.

The once state-of-the-art theater was built with vaudeville in mind, with a fancy pipe organ for silent movies and a stage for live acts. By 1928, talkies called for the installation of a sound system, and by 1938, the first Technicolor film graced the main screen.

When the golden age of cinema began to fade into the sunset, so did the Gillioz. It remained closed for several years but sparkles once again as the premier event venue in Springfield. You can always embark on a behind-the-scenes tour, however the best way to experience this slice of Springfield history is to attend a movie, concert, comedy act, play, musical, or opera. A robust performance schedule and a handful of resident companies keep the stage bursting with entertainment every night of the year.

325 Park Central E., Springfield, MO; (417) 863-9491; gillioztheatre.com

ELVIS ROOM AT THE BEST WESTERN ROUTE 66 RAIL HAVEN

In 1956, Elvis Presley headlined Springfield's 4,000-seat Shine Mosque. The at-capacity crowd adored him. Afterward, he crashed in room 409 at the Rail Haven. You can still stay in Room 409, where Elvis's ghost just might haunt you in your dreams.

When it opened for business in 1938, the Rail Haven, named after the split-rail fence that surrounded the property, was considered a premier hotel. An early post-card bragged "A motor court for motorists who demand the best." Each room featured automatic safety-controlled gas heat and a direct-dial telephone, both luxe amenities at the time. Eight bedroom-plus-kitchenette cottages, built of sandstone on 4 acres of a

Courtesy of Missouri Division of Tourism

former orchard, and an on-site, full-service gas station welcomed road-tripping guests. Cars are still welcome to pull up to the covered, Colonial-style carport for check-in at the quaint main office. Old-school gas pumps flank the main entrance. The lobby is a flashback to the '50s; reservations are still taken over the old-fashioned phone with its rotary dial.

Take your pick from 93 units; 42 of them are old-fashioned, cottage court style. Room 409 is hard to snag, but if you're an Elvis fan, reserve far in advance so you can soothe your tired travel bones in the Jacuzzi and then count sheep from the comfort of a '57 Chevy convertible bed. A Marilyn Monroe room is decked out in honor of the celluloid princess. Yet another room is dedicated to musician John Wilkinson, a former Springfield resident who played guitar for Elvis Presley in more than 1,000 shows, from 1968 until Presley's death in 1977. If you can't check into one of the precious themed rooms, request one with yet another unbeatable amenity, a vibrating recliner.

203 S. Glenstone Ave., Springfield, MO; (417) 866-1963; bestwestern.com

WILSON'S CREEK NATIONAL BATTLEFIELD PARK

Just as the early morning sun rose into the sky, on August 10, 1861, General Franz Sigel, under the command of Union Brigadier General Nathaniel Lyon, ordered 1,200 Union soldiers to attack a Confederate camp here at Wilson's Creek, sparking a bitter battle that raged on for more than five hours. The Confederates counterattacked

the Union forces three times but failed to break through the Union line and pulled back after the third attack. By 11 a.m., around 1,317 Union and 1,230 Confederate/Missourian/Arkansan soldiers were either killed, wounded, or captured in the intense fighting, including Lyon, who was killed while trying to rally his outnumbered soldiers. The exhausted Union troops retreated to Springfield, but the Confederates were too poorly equipped to pursue retreating troops. President Lincoln sent reinforcements, securing the state of Missouri for the Union.

Today, the National Park Service operates Wilson's Creek National Battlefield on the site of the first major Civil War battle fought west of the Mississippi River. Located just off Route 66 in Republic, Missouri, it's one of 16 national parks located within a 30-mile radius of the Mother Road.

You can take a tour of this Civil War battlefield, considered to be one of the three best preserved Civil War battlefields in the national park system, by car thanks to the 4.9-mile paved tour road with its eight interpretive stops at significant points, including the Ray house, a farmhouse used as a Confederate field hospital during and after the battle, Edwards Cabin, Confederate General Price's headquarters, and a wooded hill just beyond the creek, aptly named Bloody Hill, where the most savage fighting took place.

At the visitor center, a short film depicts the battle, which marked the beginning of the Civil War in Missouri, and the days leading up to it. The on-site museum displays more than 5,000 artifacts from the Trans-Mississippi Theater of the Civil War. Arranged chronologically, they range from John Brown and the 1850s to the last battle involving Missouri troops at Fort Blakely, Alabama, in April 1865. The exhibit highlighting medicine in the Civil War is especially gruesome: the amputation kit with its knives, saws, and bone nippers brings the dire treatment of choice for gunshot wounds to arms and legs to the vivid forefront.

6424 W. Farm Rd. 182, Republic, MO; (417) 732-2662; nps.gov/wicr

BOOTS COURT MOTEL

Boots Court Motel offers what few other motels these days can: an authentic 1940s motel experience. It's easy to imagine that you're stopping for the night after a long day traveling Route 66 in its heyday, when Boots was smack dab in the middle of the "Crossroads of America"—the junction of Route 66, from Chicago to LA, and Route 71, which runs from Canada to the Gulf of Mexico.

Arthur Boots opened the motel in 1939. Thirteen guest rooms welcomed guests, though the 13th room was labeled #14 because of the fear among hoteliers that the number 13 might harbor bad luck. The motel offered top-notch amenities, proudly advertising "a radio in every room," tile showers, floor furnaces with thermostat control, and air conditioners. The Streamline Moderne building is a clean, crisp white, its roofline and walls accented in black Carrara glass and green neon; a red-and-white neon sign attracted passersby. Each guest room included a covered carport. This was the ritziest motel in Carthage. Even Clark Gable stayed here—in Room #10—whenever he came to Carthage to visit his wartime buddy.

Courtesy of Boots Court Motel

In the mid-1940s, Arthur Boots capitalized on the motel's success and opened a drive-in diner across the street, offering fountain service and "breakfast at any hour." KDMO 1490 AM broadcast on-location interviews with many of the travelers passing through from faraway places in the popular radio show "Breakfast at the Crossroads of America."

Ultimately Interstate 44 diverted traffic 7 miles south of the town, and the diner closed in 1971 while the Boots, as it is affectionately known, entered a slow, sad decline.

But in 2011, sisters Deborah Harvey and Priscilla Bledsaw breathed life back into the Boots by lovingly carrying the court motel back to its 1940s splendor. They tore off the hideous, 1970s gabled rooftop and restored the characteristic flat roof. They refurnished the rooms in authentic period decor, polishing chrome light fixtures, refurbishing built-in dressers, and returning an old-time radio to each. The duo also organized the beautiful restoration of the neon sign by the original sign maker, thanks to a $2,500 donation from Ron Jones, an Oklahoma man best known for tattooing more than 80 Route 66 landmarks on his body. When the sisters reopened the motel in 2012, Bob Boots, the son of the original owners, now in his eighties, was the first guest of the restored Boots Court at the 1940s price of $2.50 per night.

The Harvey Sisters have happily seen their Route 66 dreams come true: "Serendipity drew us to Boots Court," explains Deborah Harvey. "My sister and I did a Route 66 trip in 2006 and came by the Boots when it was looking neglected and dejected. It was empty at the time. We thought it would probably be torn down, so we took its picture 'for the historical record,' and, for the rest of the trip, talked about how much fun it would be to actually own a motel on Route 66 and get to sit out in front of it and wave at the passersby and meet all the interesting people traveling the Route. We did NOT discuss how much work that would be, however, mostly because we didn't know!

"When the Boots came up for sale five years later, in 2011, my sister and I decided to buy it because we thought we might not get another chance to realize that fantasy of owning a Route 66 motel. We did not realize at the time what a worldwide icon the Boots was, even then. We found that out later as people from all over the world stopped by to take its picture even before we had any rooms available.

"I have a masters in heritage preservation, with a specialty in historic buildings, and I thought it would be fun to put the Boots back the way it was in its heyday and use it to show modern travelers something of what it was like to run the Route in the 1940s. So, in addition to being an amenity on the Route, we use it as a teaching tool—we conduct tours of the property for anyone who wants one, whether they are staying at the Boots or not, and tell them the history of the buildings as we know it (it has changed over the years as we find out more about it), and something about traveling during the historic period, the heyday of Route 66."

107 S. Garrison Ave., Carthage, MO; (417) 310-2989; bootsmotel.homestead.com

BONNIE AND CLYDE'S GARAGE HIDEOUT 📷

Bonnie and Clyde roamed the southwestern United States during the height of the Great Depression, from 1932 to 1934, leaving murder and mayhem in the wake of their numerous armed robberies. Though the press painted the pair as lovelorn lawbreakers, the duo, along with their gang of like-minded criminals, killed at least 13 people during their time together, including two police officers.

Bonnie Parker was born in Texas in 1910. At 16 years old, Bonnie was married to a man who would be sentenced to 99 years in prison for robbery just one year after their marriage. When Clyde Barrow, already a hardened criminal who had served time in his home state of Texas, waltzed into her life, she was instantly smitten. Together the pair became the first celebrity criminals of the modern era.

On April 1, 1933, after a long spree of robberies in Missouri and neighboring states, Bonnie and Clyde rented the unassuming garage apartment in the small, stone Craftsman-style building located here at 3347½ Oak Ridge Drive in Joplin. For 12 days the duo and their gang hid out, until neighbors, suspicious of the secretive renters' rowdy card parties and their out-of-state license plates, notified the police. On April 13, the Joplin Police Department raided the apartment. Two police officers were killed in the ensuing machine gun shootout.

Bonnie and Clyde barely managed to escape, leaving most of their possessions behind. In the three months that followed, they traveled as far north as Minnesota. The crimes they committed along their wayward journey became increasingly cold-blooded. A little more than a year after the Joplin raid, on May 23, 1934, Bonnie and Clyde's

murderous spree came to an end in a hailstorm of bullets when they were shot by police officers in rural Louisiana.

Bonnie fancied herself a poet, and in the autobiographical poem titled "The End of the Line," written shortly before her death, she remarked:

> They don't think they're too smart or desperate;
> They know the law always wins;
> They've been shot at before;
> But they do not ignore that death is the wages of sin.
> Someday they'll go down together;
> And they'll bury them side by side;
> To a few it'll be grief—

To the law a relief—

But it's death for Bonnie and Clyde.

A marker in front of the building details its unfortunate history. The Garage Hideout is currently private property, so be mindful of the homeowners when snapping photos. You can see firsthand all the things that Bonnie and Clyde left behind as they fled their Joplin apartment at the Joplin Historical Museum (504 S. Schifferdecker Ave., Joplin) including a camera with some of the iconic photos that were subsequently developed from it, Bonnie's costume jewelry, and even the former front door, which remains riddled with bullet holes.

3347½ Oak Ridge Dr., Joplin, MO

KANSAS

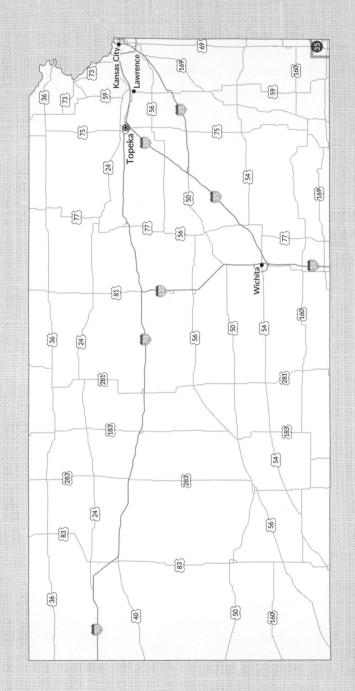

Kansas City
Lawrence

Topeka

Wichita

35 Kan-O-Tex Service Station

KANSAS

US

66

KAN-O-TEX SERVICE STATION 📷

It's hard not to love goofy, good old Tow Mater, "the world's best backwards driver," star of the 2006 Pixar movie *Cars*. In the movie, Mater owned his very own towing and salvage company in rural Radiator Springs, a fictional town based on multiple Historic Route 66 stopping points. In real life, he likely would have lived here at the Kan-O-Tex Service Station in the mining town of Galena, Kansas. The 1951 International Harvester L-170 truck parked at this former filling station and automobile repair shop, built in 1934 to service the many motorists passing through town along the route, was the inspiration for loveable, bucked-tooth Tow Mater.

Galena is named for its most prized attribute, galena, a lead sulfide ore that was mined here from 1877 to the 1970s. By 1929, the entirety of the small segment of

Patti/Flickr.com

PIT STOP PHOTO OP

Take your souvenir selfie with Tow Mater, star of Disney/Pixar's *Cars* franchise and "the world's best backwards driver."

Route 66 that passes through Kansas, and likewise Galena, boasted pavement, a distinction that only one other state—Illinois—had earned; similar service stations sprouted seemingly overnight.

In 1979, US 66 was rerouted, bypassing the station and cutting off its customers.

In 2007, three local ladies restored the abandoned station and its sign, a five-point star backed by a sunflower, the logo of Kanotex Refining Company, a regional fuel brand, now extinct, named for Kansas, Oklahoma, and Texas. The picturesque pumps no longer provide actual fuel, and a diner-style lunch counter and souvenir shop now occupy the station's repair garage. Tow Mater is parked outside, ready and waiting for photo ops.

Pixar sent a group of fifteen artists off to explore Route 66 to gather inspiration before creating *Cars*. A Disney/Pixar crew returned here to film an interview with the station's owners, which appears on the DVD release of *Cars 2*. Producer John Lasseter was also inspired by Galena's historic Front Street Garage, where faded yet iconic advertising murals can still be seen on its north side.

119 N. Main St., Galena, KS; (620) 783-1366

OKLAHOMA

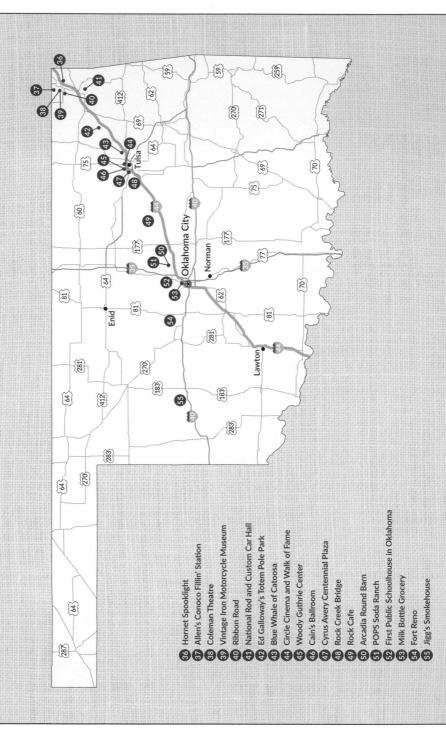

36 Hornet Spooklight
37 Allen's Conoco Fillin' Station
38 Coleman Theatre
39 Vintage Iron Motorcycle Museum
40 Ribbon Road
41 National Rod and Custom Car Hall
42 Ed Galloway's Totem Pole Park
43 Blue Whale of Catoosa
44 Circle Cinema and Walk of Fame
45 Woody Guthrie Center
46 Cain's Ballroom
47 Cyrus Avery Centennial Plaza
48 Rock Creek Bridge
49 Rock Cafe
50 Arcadia Round Barn
51 POPS Soda Ranch
52 First Public Schoolhouse in Oklahoma
53 Milk Bottle Grocery
54 Fort Reno
55 Jigg's Smokehouse

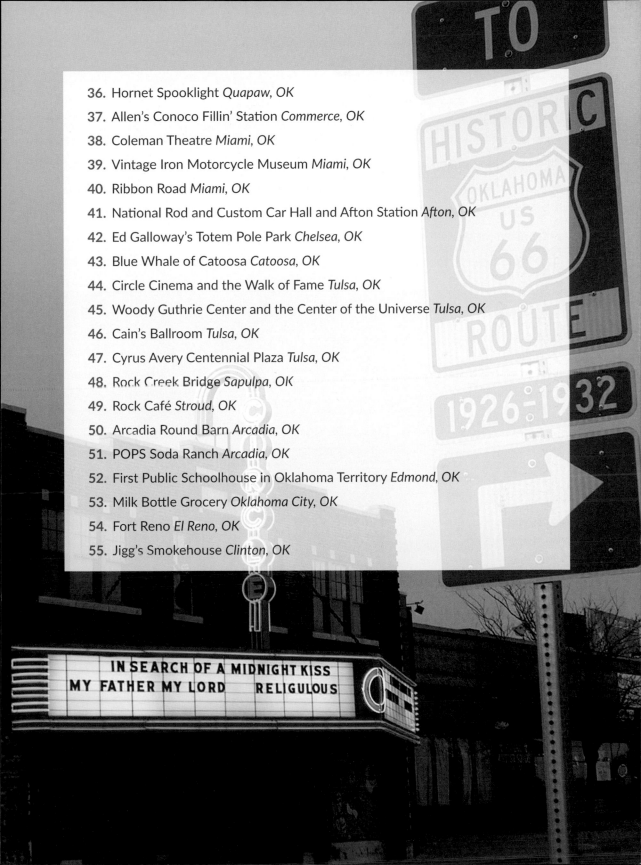

HORNET SPOOKLIGHT

It's the scariest tract of Route 66, with a name to match. The so-called Devil's Promenade is a mysterious, 4-mile rural road in the tiny hamlet of Hornet, Missouri, about 12
miles southwest of Joplin, Missouri. If you're lucky—or better yet, unlucky—you might
spot a bizarre orange orb, the size of a basketball, glowing in the darkness of the night.

The Hornet Spooklight has puzzlingly popped up out of nothingness since it was
first spotted in 1866. Even the US Army Corps of Engineers have concluded that it's a
"mysterious light of unknown origin." No one knows what this peculiar, smoldering ball

of light signifies, where it comes from, or what it's composed of. It moves, spinning and bobbing up and down, like a lantern held by a dancing ghost, and is usually spotted from inside the Oklahoma border looking to the west. Almost as if it were a sort of apparition, it always appears out of nowhere and disappears into thin air when approached.

Local legends, which reach back to the 1800s, state that the light is the spirit of a decapitated Osage Indian chief, who is forever searching for his missing head, lantern in hand, or the ghost of a father, forever searching for his missing children.

Theories abound. Could it be "marsh gas," a sometimes spontaneously combustible brew of methane, hydrogen sulfide, and carbon dioxide? Perhaps it emanates from minerals present in the area electrical fields, created by tiny earthquakes. Or maybe they are altogether something less haunting and simply the reflection of headlights from cars rambling down the nearby highway.

A trek to catch the eerie Hornet Spooklight is worth the patience. Park your car in the field on the side of the road and wait quietly in the darkness.

From I-44, take exit 4 onto Highway 86 South. Follow for about 6 miles, to junction Route BB. Turn right on BB Highway and follow the road until it ends. Turn right again, go 1 mile, and turn left onto E50 Road, a.k.a. Spooklight Road.

ALLEN'S CONOCO FILLIN' STATION 🖼️

During the Mother Road's magical early years, these two cozy cottages, both located on Commerce's main drag, likely competed for business.

Allen's Conoco Fillin' Station is the cutest little gas station in Oklahoma. The adorable red-and-green painted brick cottage, with its two old-fashioned pumps standing proudly at the forefront, was built sometime between 1929 and 1930 to service drivers traveling along the newly paved Route 66. Best known as the "Hole in the Wall Conoco Station," it truly is a hole-in-the-wall: it was constructed outward from the exterior wall

of a large brick building. It closed when Route 66 lost its edge to other, larger highways but was lovingly restored and transformed into a tiny souvenir shop.

Just across Main Street, the majestic Dairy King is yet another historic, cottage-style vintage gas station. It still sports its original look yet is now a quick-serve roadside restaurant, with burgers and custard-style ice cream on the menu, instead of the original Marathon gas.

Before you head out of town, fuel up on the Dairy King's regal, Route 66 sign–shape cookies, available in plain sugar and chocolate chip, which are baked in-house.

101 S. Main St., Commerce, OK

COLEMAN THEATRE 👞

On April 18, 1929, local zinc and lead mining magnate George Coleman presented the small town of Miami, Oklahoma, with a gift like no other. Wrapped up in a grand, stuccoed Spanish Revival exterior, with fine terra-cotta detailing, arched, stained glass windows, and wrought-iron ornamentation, and capped with bell towers and balconettes, the Coleman Theatre brought with it the intoxicating air of the world beyond Main Street America. The first locals to enter the elegant Louis XV interior, which displayed all the elements of the finest palace, including gold-leaf trim, marble accents, and a grand mahogany staircase, were quite simply dazzled.

Lori Duckworth/Oklahoma Tourism

Like many theaters at the time, the Coleman first hosted vaudeville acts, then transitioned to silent movies, and finally talkies. The biggest stars of stage and screen all appeared on the Coleman's stage, from burlesque babe Sally Rand to Bing Crosby, from Olympic gold medalist Jim Thorpe to master magician Harry Blackstone. Motorists traveling along the recently designated US Highway 66 made a point of stopping here to catch a show at the theater billed the most elaborate entertainment facility between Dallas and Kansas City.

Restored to all its 1920s splendor soon after the Coleman family donated the building to the city, the theater still stands as one of the most magnificent on Route 66. The theater offers free tours in addition to its robust schedule of movies, concerts, and plays. Try to catch a silent movie screening, always accompanied by the theater's gigantic vintage pipe organ, nicknamed the "Mighty Wurlitzer."

103 N. Main St., Miami, OK; (918) 540-2425; colemantheatre.org

VINTAGE IRON MOTORCYCLE MUSEUM 📷

Route 66 is the ultimate bucket list ride for any motorcycle enthusiast. It's a journey back in time, made all the better when soaking in the freedom of the open road from the comfort of a Harley.

Whether you're riding your dream motorcycle along the Mother Road, or stuck in a minivan yet still dreaming of the day you can get your hands on a chopper, a stop at the Route 66 Vintage Iron Motorcycle Museum, located on the Mother Road in downtown Miami, is a motorcyclist must-do.

All 2,000 square feet of this small museum is packed with motorcycles and motorcycle memorabilia. More than 40 vintage motorcycles on display include a 1917 Harley Davidson, a 1972 Yamaha world-record jump bike, a 2004 Honda world-record jump bike, a 1949 Indian Scout, a 1949 AJS, and a 1957 Ariel Red Hunter. It also houses the largest vintage motorcycle photo collection in the country.

If you're an Evel Knievel fan, an ever-growing cache of Evel Knievel memorabilia rounds out this fabulous collection, including the actual Mission Control Super Van he used in his (failed) attempt to jump Idaho's Snake River Canyon in 1974.

In addition to the museum's artifacts, everything a motorcyclist needs to hit the road, in style, is available for sale, including gloves, goggles, helmets, and an outstanding selection of T-shirts with logos of motorcycle manufacturers from days gone by.

128 S. Main St., Miami, OK; (918) 542-6170; route66vintageiron.com

RIBBON ROAD 📷

It's one of the most vintage pieces of pavement along old Route 66, a zigzagging 6.5 miles of Topeka asphalt through the ranchlands that run between Miami and Afton, Oklahoma. But don't count on driving your semi down this portion of America's byway

as it is more suitable for a toy truck. Ribbon Road isn't much bigger than a sidewalk, at 9 feet wide; hence it's other nickname, "Sidewalk Highway."

It was built before Route 66, in the early 1920s, and legend has it that Oklahoma, which had just entered the union in 1907, was in high need of a roadway yet short on cash. Instead of cutting costs, they cut the width of the planned highway in half. In 1926, it morphed into Route 66. In 1937, Route 66 was realigned and much of the original sidewalk highway is now buried under OK 59, save for this small stretch. Prepare yourself for a bumpy ride: the Ribbon Road offers a true taste of early driving conditions on the Mother Road.

From downtown Miami, go south on Main Street from the US 69–OK 10 intersection for about 3 miles to a T intersection. The Sidewalk Highway begins at the right and eventually rejoins US 69.

NATIONAL ROD AND CUSTOM CAR HALL AND AFTON STATION 📷

Afton, Oklahoma, has always been a welcoming refuge for car enthusiasts. Before Route 66 carried an influx of motorists to its picturesque Main Street, stagecoaches and buggies breezed through the small town on their way west. The Pierce & Harvey Buggy Company, located in a building that still stands at the corner of 1st Street and South Main Avenue, repaired and manufactured horse-drawn buggies. Years later, American custom car and hot rod designer and builder Darryl Starbird began manufacturing cars with mid-century designs so futuristic and fantastic they seem to be ready to ride on the ridges of the moon. Today, Starbird owns and operates the National Rod and Custom

Car Hall of Fame Museum in Afton, a one-of-a-kind museum that celebrates the history of custom car and hot rod culture

Darryl, a.k.a. "King of the Bubbletop," began cranking out his specialty cars in 1954, when the art of customizing was still brand new. It's no surprise that he studied aeronautical engineering in college at Wichita State. At his unique museum, more than 50 of the hottest, most fast-forward cars ever made rest on 80 acres of lakefront in a parklike setting. Highlights include Starbird's signature Predicta with its Lucite bubble top and mesmerizing taillights and the space-age Reactor Mach II, which you might recognize as the "Jupiter 8," a two-seat sports car marketed to the inhabitants of the planet 892-IV. The green-and-gold Reactor Mach II was Catwoman's slick getaway vehicle of choice. Note that the museum is closed November through February, as most of the cars are displayed outdoors.

55251 OK-85A, Afton, OK; (918) 257-4234; darrylstarbird.com

Wikimedia Commons

Afton's Eagle D-X filling station opened in 1934 as the first-ever 24-hour service station along the Mother Road. Today it's the Afton Station Packard Museum, a privately owned museum housing 18 beautifully restored Packards, American automobiles produced from 1899 to 1956. Note the authentic D-X fuel pumps at the station's forecourt and the "Approved Packard Service" dealership logo atop the large signpost. The station also serves as an unofficial welcome center distributing maps, guidebooks, Route 66 doo-dads, and sage advice for the road.

12 SE 1st St., Afton, OK; (918) 284-3829; aftonstationroute66.com

ED GALLOWAY'S TOTEM POLE PARK 📷

Veer 3.5 miles off the Mother Road and you'll encounter a 90-foot-tall sandstone totem pole, perched on a turtle-shape base, surrounded by other, smaller totem poles adorned with birds, trees, arrowheads, and other Native American motifs. No, you haven't accidentally steered your car off Route 66 and into the Pacific Northwest. You're in rural Foyil, Oklahoma, a town with a population hovering a pinch below 400. And unlike traditional totem poles, which were typically carved from western red cedar trees by the indigenous peoples that once lived in today's Washington, Oregon, and British Columbia, these

Lori Duckworth/Oklahoma Tourism

particular totem poles are crafted in stone or concrete reinforced with steel rebar and wood.

Born in Springfield, Missouri, in 1880, Nathan Edward Galloway taught himself the art of wood carving as a young boy. Later, he taught the trade to orphan boys. After his retirement in 1937, he dedicated himself to building Totem Pole Park, a unique property inspired by his interest in Native American culture. Though Oklahoma is home to several indigenous nations, none of them has a significant totem pole tradition, so Galloway studied postcards and perused *National Geographic* magazines then constructed his multifaceted totem poles in the grassy field surrounding his "Fiddle House," an 11-sided building that re-creates a Navajo hogan and houses his hand-carved fiddles.

After Galloway's death in the early 1960s, the park fell into disrepair. Thankfully, the Rogers County Historical Society acquired and restored it in the late 1980s. Today it stands as the largest open-air folk art museum in the state.

Galloway, perhaps mindful of the day when his park would be visited by travelers from around the world, also designed colorful concrete tables and chairs in his trade-mark style, making the park an ideal stopping point for a picnic lunch.

21310 E. Hwy. 28A, Chelsea, OK; (918) 283-8035; rchs1.org/totem-pole-park

BLUE WHALE OF CATOOSA 📷

It's the least likely place you'd expect to find a beached, blue whale. In tiny Catoosa, Oklahoma, an 80-foot-long sperm whale smiles, stranded on land beside a swimming hole. How did this magnificent creature end up so far from his ocean home?

The Blue Whale of Catoosa is one of the most beloved and quirky attractions along Route 66. Hand-built of pipe and concrete, it boasts a diving board of a tail and a slide protruding from its head. In 1972, Hugh Davis, one-time director of the Tulsa Zoo, surprised his family by creating the turquoise whale as a wedding anniversary gift for his wife. A few years later, the family transformed their whale of a backyard into Nature's

Acres, a reptile petting zoo. The spring-fed pond and its resident sperm whale attracted visitors from near and far.

According to daughter Dee Dee, Hugh Davis "believed that every day was a beautiful day, that people should use the talents God gave them, that one should keep busy by thinking, planning, and creating, that people should love what they do and do what they love, that you should always finish what you start and that you should enjoy life and live it to its fullest." The blue whale encapsulates this wonderful outlook on life.

Then the Davis kids grew up, the petting zoo closed, the once-swimmable pond found itself coated with a thick layer of pond scum, and the blue whale began a slow decline towards that great ocean in the sky.

Thankfully the blue whale was saved by the fine citizens of landlocked Catoosa, his concrete patched up, his blubber coated with fresh, brilliant blue paint. Today, the Blue Whale of Catoosa remains forever poised, fishhook just within reach of his bright red lips, to be the big catch of the day.

While visitors can no longer dive into the pond and take a swim, it's still possible to climb a small ladder into the brain of the beast.

2600 Route 66, Catoosa, OK; bluewhaleroute66.com

CIRCLE CINEMA AND THE WALK OF FAME 📷

On July 15, 1928, Hollywood officially arrived in Tulsa when the Circle Theatre opened its doors and the silent movie *Across the Atlantic* brought the golden age of Hollywood to its single screen. Located on the original alignment of Route 66 at Lewis Avenue, just south of Admiral Boulevard, this classic neighborhood movie theater housed in a humble, two-story brick commercial-style building attracted both locals and visitors with its bright neon sign and marquee. But it was the movies that made Circle Cinema the star of Tulsa.

The history of Hollywood parallels the history of this, the oldest cinema in Tulsa.

Courtesy of Circle Cinema Foundation, Inc.

The theater witnessed the sunset of the silent movie era, saying goodbye to its beloved pipe organ and hello to the talkies. The cinema flourished as Hollywood began cranking out blockbuster after blockbuster. It wasn't until the advent of television and home videos that business began to decline. By 1978, the classic movie theater was screening adult films just to stay alive; by the mid-nineties, it went dark for a decade. Thankfully, a group of local movie-house buffs worked to restore the theater—even the Circle's original 1928 theater pipe organ was repurchased, refurbished, and reinstalled—and in 2003 it reopened as a nonprofit, art house cinema offering an innovative mix of programming, showcasing both classic and contemporary films with an uplifting mission: to create community consciousness through film.

On the sidewalk just outside the theater, the Circle Cinema Walk of Fame honors Oklahoma-born film legends with circular, granite stepping stones. James Garner, Tony Randall, Gene Autry, Joan Crawford, and Brad Pitt are just a few of the featured celebrities with ties to the Sooner State.

You might recognize the Circle Cinema from the opening scene of the 1983 hit *The Outsiders*, when Ponyboy exits the iconic theater. Author S. E. Hinton, a Tulsa native, wrote the novel that inspired the movie when she was a teenager herself; she too is honored with a marker on the walk of fame.

10 S. Lewis Ave., Tulsa, OK; (918) 585-3504; circlecinema.com

WOODY GUTHRIE CENTER AND THE CENTER OF THE UNIVERSE 📷

No other singer encapsulates the spirit of Route 66 better than Woody Guthrie. Considered one of the most important and influential American folk singer–songwriters, his social justice–themed music inspired countless travelers along the Mother Road as well as hundreds of musicians who blossomed in his wake.

Born on July 14, 1912, in Okemah, Oklahoma, he was forced to leave his young wife and three children when severe dust storms engulfed the surrounding prairies during the tragic Dust Bowl of the 1930s. Guthrie was just one of thousands of the so-called Okies who traveled along Route 66 to California in search of work.

Guthrie's music offered hope and strength to the struggling. He never shied away from sharing his social and political values. His most famous song, "This Land Is Your

Land," recorded in 1944, sings the joys of the Mother Road journey while also serving as a powerful reminder that America's beauty belongs to each and every citizen:

> As I went walking that ribbon of highway
> I saw above me that endless skyway
> And saw below me that golden valley
> This land was made for you and me
> I roamed and rambled and I followed my footsteps
> To the sparkling sands of her diamond deserts
> And all around me, a voice was sounding
> This land was made for you and me
> When the sun comes shining, then I was strolling
> In the wheat fields waving and dust clouds rolling
> The voice was chanting as the fog was lifting
> This land was made for you and me.

The Woody Guthrie Center strives to promote and preserve the legacy of this American cultural icon. The Center's Woody Guthrie Archive serves as a repository for Guthrie's prolific writings, art, and songs. Located among the many former warehouses in the historic Brady Arts District, one of Tulsa's oldest neighborhoods, this former home of the Tulsa Paper Company houses the world's largest collection of material relating to Guthrie's life. Especially poignant are the interactive displays that showcase Guthrie's fiddle and his handwritten lyrics. Take a moment to view the short film that summarizes the star's rich life story and try to plan your visit around one of the center's many live music performances. You just might catch a rising folk-singing star.

102 E. Mathew B. Brady St., Tulsa, OK; (918) 574-2710; woodyguthriecenter.org

It's hard to believe, but the Center of the Universe is just a short, two-minute walk from the Woody Guthrie Center, and you won't need a rocket ship to get there: walk on over to the pedestrian overpass along Boston Ave between Archer and 1st Streets to the brick circle.

Stand at the very center of the circle—it doesn't matter what direction you face—and whisper, shout, or sing: your voice will hit the nearby concrete walls and echo back to you even louder. Though some claim that this mysterious spot in Tulsa is a vortex where all the cosmic energies of the universe collide, the phenomenon's explanation is simple: the bridge that you're standing on features a circular design and the intriguing echo is the result of the parabolic reflectivity of the circular planter walls that partly surround the circle.

Located on the pedestrian overpass that runs along Boston Ave between Archer and 1st Streets. The closest address is 50 S. Boston Ave., Tulsa.

CAIN'S BALLROOM

If you haven't stepped out onto the spring-loaded dance floor at Cain's, you haven't lived. This historic ballroom has hosted *all* the legends, from the Texas Playboys to the Sex Pistols. Every single genre of music—jazz, rag, country, new wave, rock, punk, funk,

Lori Duckworth/Oklahoma Tourism

heavy metal, boogie, blues, big band, and swing—has been welcomed with open arms and dancing feet on the epic dance floor.

This beloved ballroom, considered one of the top performance venues in the world today, began its life as a humble garage when Tulsa entrepreneur Tate Brady built it all the way back in 1924, to house his automobiles. In the 1930s, Madison W. "Daddy" Cain purchased the building and turned it into Cain's Dance Academy, charging a whopping 10 cents for dance lessons. Then Bob Wills, the King of Western Swing, and his band, the Texas Playboys, transformed it into the best live music venue in Tulsa when they began performing on a regular basis, extending their fame country-wide by hosting their own in-house radio show. More acts followed over the years, their faces forever memorialized in the oversize photographs that line the walls.

The best way to experience Cain's Ballroom is to swing with your sweetheart on the springy maple-wood dance floor with its log cabin–style squares that are known to vibrate and shake along with the foot stomping, toe tapping, screaming, and spinning. The programming remains delightfully eclectic, so you never know who your ears will encounter in this legendary music hall. Cain's Ballroom still sells more tickets to more shows than any other club venue in Oklahoma so be sure to order your tickets well in advance.

423 N. Main St., Tulsa, OK; (918) 584-2306; cainsballroom.com

CYRUS AVERY CENTENNIAL PLAZA 🔟

Cyrus Avery was a highway visionary. Buoyed by his belief that an interstate highway would be a boon to his hometown of Tulsa, the entrepreneur-of-all-trades was a member of several road infrastructure–focused associations. He played a key role in the construction of the 11th Street Bridge across the Arkansas River, the creation of the Ozark Trail highway, which connected St. Louis, Missouri, and Amarillo, Texas, and the implementation of a gasoline tax to fund the construction of more highways across the state of Oklahoma.

While serving on the Joint Board of Interstate Highways, Avery worked to create new federal highways. Congress requested a highway that ran from Virginia Beach, Virginia, to Los Angeles, California, following today's US Highway 60, but Avery proposed a road that ran south through Tulsa and Oklahoma City, continuing west across Texas, New Mexico, Arizona, and Southern California, following commercial routes already in place and avoiding the tricky peaks of the Rocky Mountains. As the father of Route 66, Avery helped establish the US Highway 66 Association, which both promoted the new highway and pushed for its pavement from start to finish. US 66 was officially signed into law on November 11, 1926, as one of the original US highways, though road signs didn't pop up until the following year, and it wasn't completely paved until 1938.

Located on the Old 11th Street Bridge, the Cyrus Avery Centennial Plaza, completed in 2008, honors the Father of Route 66 with an enormous bronze statue that captures Avery himself at the wheel of a Model T. As he climbs out of his car to help a farmer in a horse-drawn carriage, Avery's wife Essie turns to check on their daughter, who is seated in the backseat trying to settle her startled kitty cat. Created by Texas artist Robert Summers and cast by the Deep in the Heart Art Foundry in Bastrop, Texas, the sculpture captures the collision of the past and future along the Mother Road. See if you can spot the bronze grasshopper smashed onto the Model T's grill.

Old 11th Street Bridge, Southwest Boulevard at Riverside Drive, Tulsa, OK

ROCK CREEK BRIDGE

Motorists traveling along the newly branded Route 66 approached the Rock Creek Bridge with awe. Constructed in 1924 by the Concrete & Steel Construction Company of Joplin, Missouri, with a total span of 146 feet and a 17-foot deck width, the steel-truss bridge was considered ultramodern in its early years. Crossing the eponymous

Wikimedia Commons/Sara Carter

creek that flowed beneath, it was built as part of the old Ozark Trail, which became part of Route 66 in 1926 and served the Mother Road until it was realigned to the south in the early 1950s. Today it's one of a handful of remaining steel-truss bridges in Oklahoma, though it's no longer traversable by automobile.

Before steel-truss bridges popped up across rivers throughout the US, wooden-beam bridges, which couldn't support much weight, carried coaches and early cars over shallow rivers and creeks. Then came truss bridges with their steel beams, which could handle heavier loads and extend over deeper waters.

Walk across the unique, red-brick pavement of this beautiful old bridge to experience the same picturesque views of the slow-flowing creek and its tree-lined banks that early Route 66 motorists marveled at when crossing the once-modern bridge.

Junction of US 66 and West Ozark Trail, Sapulpa, OK

ROCK CAFÉ ⊚

Rock Café fired up its determined grill, "Betsy," for business way back in August 1939. Owner Roy Rives took three years to painstakingly build his aptly named Rock Café out of a load of local colorful sandstone, leftovers from a recent route construction, that he had purchased for just $5. Traffic boomed along Route 66, as the US slowly emerged from the Great Depression, and the Rock Café became a popular place to fuel up on eggs, bacon, toast, pancakes—all the American breakfast favorites you can imagine—and of course, ever-flowing coffee. During World War II, a steady stream of GIs popped in as they traveled to and fro on home leave, as the café was a designated Greyhound bus line stop.

Despite a major tornado in 1999 and a fire in 2008, as well as a loss of business from cross-country travelers when Interstate 44 stole most of Route 66's traffic, Rock Café somehow manages to retain its original atmosphere: It's still capped with the same green tin roof; drivers are still attracted by the bright neon sign, and the giraffe-style

sandstones hold the whole diner together in all their rocky glory. Even the original layout of the main dining room remains unchanged, and Betsy is still hard at work: Over the years, she has seared more than five million burgers. As the owners lovingly explain, "When asked what is the favorite food at the Rock Café, we say: anything coming off Betsy."

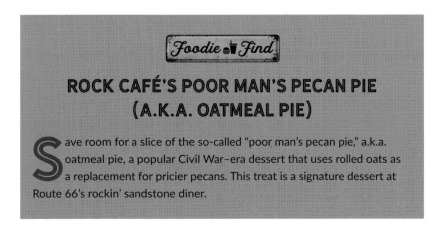

Foodie 🥤 *Find*

ROCK CAFÉ'S POOR MAN'S PECAN PIE (A.K.A. OATMEAL PIE)

Save room for a slice of the so-called "poor man's pecan pie," a.k.a. oatmeal pie, a popular Civil War–era dessert that uses rolled oats as a replacement for pricier pecans. This treat is a signature dessert at Route 66's rockin' sandstone diner.

Betsy is best known for cooking up all your stick-to-the-ribs diner favorites, including ham and beans, chicken-fried steak with mashed potatoes and fried okra, and burgers and fried pickle slices, but give some of the more unusual house-made specials a try, including the American take on a German classic—spaetzle and cheese—and the ranch cowboy candy (onion strings and jalapeño rings lightly breaded and deep-fried).

114 W. Main St., Stroud, OK; (918) 968-3990; rockcafert66.com

ARCADIA ROUND BARN 🔟

Perched just above the scenic Deep Forge River, the Round Barn of Arcadia celebrates the sublime over the simply functional.

William Harrison Oder, a.k.a. "Big Bill," went big . . . and round . . . when it came to the construction of his barn, which began all the way back in 1898. He built the foundation of local red Permian rock and then soaked burr oak timbers in water until they were soft enough to bend into a round barn that rose to a height of 43 feet with an ambitious 60-foot diameter.

The barn was so beautiful upon completion that three of the young men who helped raise it declared it a dance hall, effectively persuading Big Bill to install dancing feet–friendly hardwood floors. Hence the barn not only welcomed grain, hay, and cattle but also up-and-coming area musicians and crowds of dancing locals. Music always seemed to be reverberating through the rounded rafters.

Though you can no longer take your sweetheart to a dance in this the only truly round barn in the US—not hexagonal or octagonal, but *round*—it remains open daily for tourists traveling along old Route 66. A small gift shop sells trinkets and other Route 66 and Round Barn–themed gifts. Every second Sunday of the month, music returns to the accidentally acoustic barn thanks to a popular concert series.

107 OK 66, Arcadia, OK; (405) 396-0824; arcadiaroundbarn.com

POPS SODA RANCH ⦿

Just outside Oklahoma City, a 66-foot-tall, 4-ton, color-shifting LED sculpture soda pop bottle stands as a syrupy sweet beacon of hope for thirsty travelers with adventuresome taste buds. At POPS Soda Ranch, the unofficial soda pop mecca of America, there's a pop flavor to fit every taste—from apple to kumquat to . . . bacon and . . . buffalo wing. Over 700 varieties of soda, arranged by color, line the shelves and walls of this modern glass building, their effervescent colors creating a stained-glass effect in a house that worships sugary refreshments.

You'll never meet this many bizarre flavors: In addition to classic sodas from across the US and around the world, you'll find every fruit flavor under the sun. Sip from a selection of over 60 ginger ales or choose from dozens upon dozens of flavored colas. The sugar rush at this nonanimal-raising ranch comes on fast and furious.

The "Sodasgusting" freezer if by far the most intriguing: It's packed with soda POPS with disgusting names yet allegedly addictive flavors. Don't let the names fool you: some of these flavors, including Bug Barf, Dragon Drool, Pimple Pop, Swamp Pop, and Pirate Piss, only sound horrific. Other flavors featured in the Sodasgusting freezer— think ranch dressing, spruce, beef jerky, and dandelion—call for truly open-minded soda pop lovers.

Soda pop also POPS up on the menu of the in-house POPS Restaurant. Wash down all your diner favorites with a bottomless fountain soda pop or even better, a hand-dipped float.

Originally owned by the late Oklahoman oil and gas magnate Aubrey McClendon, it's no surprise that you can also fill up your gas tank at one of the many pumps located under the soaring cantilever roof.

660 OK 66, Arcadia, OK; (405) 928-7677; POPS66.com

FIRST PUBLIC SCHOOLHOUSE IN OKLAHOMA TERRITORY 📷

The town of Edmond, like many others in the booming Oklahoma Territory, sprang up at high noon on April 22, 1889, when an estimated 50,000 people gathered for their chance to grab a homestead from a newly available two million acres. As the town's population swelled, 15 local ladies created the Ladies School Aid Society, marking the first official effort to create a public school for the many new resident children.

Courtesy of Edmond Historic Preservation Trust

One lady in particular, Jennie Forster, would not take no for an answer when it came to the local children's education: she marched into Brown's Lumber Company one summer day in 1889 and placed an order for lumber, on credit, to build the first public schoolhouse in Oklahoma Territory. To pay back the lumber bill, Forster went from door to door asking for donations. Not everyone shared her lofty goal: According to the Edmond Historical Society, Forster later remarked that area businessmen "felt like running out the back door when they saw me entering the front door" as she tried to garner financial support.

Built later that year, Edmond's Territorial Schoolhouse was the earliest one-room schoolhouse in the Oklahoma Territory, responsible for shaping the lives of countless children while also paving the way for public education in the eventual state of Oklahoma. Funds were also gathered to pay a schoolteacher, Miss Ollie McCormick, $75 a month for that first winter term.

When the student population outgrew the tiny schoolhouse, it was abandoned and eventually morphed into a camera shop. Then the city set its mind on bringing this historical time machine back to its original 1889 appearance.

To step into this picture-perfect schoolhouse is to step back in time to the days when children of all ages were grouped together in one room, learning the basics of reading, writing, and arithmetic under the command of a single local school teacher. The typical school day was 9 a.m. to 4 p.m., with morning and afternoon recesses of 15 minutes each and an hour period for lunch. Boys sat on one side of the room and girls on the other, while any badly behaving students sat in a corner with a dunce cap. Students worked together to gather water and wood for the stove.

The Schoolhouse is open to the public the first two Saturdays of each month from 1 to 4 p.m. and by appointment. Representatives from the Edmond Historic Preservation Trust, owners of the schoolhouse, lead guided tours, too, which can be scheduled via the Edmond Historical Society.

24 E. 2nd St., Edmond, OK; (405) 715-1889; edmondhistory.org/1889-territorial-schoolhouse

MILK BOTTLE GROCERY 📷

Traveling along Route 66's original Oklahoma City alignment, you'd have to be as blind as a bat to miss the giant milk bottle perched on top of a postage stamp–size red brick building. No doubt a tall glass of milk is the first thing that comes to mind when passing by this oversize milk bottle, built in 1948 by the local dairy industry to drum up sales.

Surprisingly, the 350-square-foot building, located in a corner lot, only served as

Wikimedia Commons/Curtis Blackburn

a grocery store for a few years in the course of its 80-year existence: it's also been, among other things, a dry-cleaning shop, a realty office, a barbecue joint, and a Vietnamese sandwich shop. Yet none of the various owners had the heart to take down the beloved milk bottle. Added to the National Register of Historic Places in 1998, the building today remains vacant, though locals are hopeful that yet another business with take shape in the triangular space.

2426 N. Classen Blvd.,
Oklahoma City, OK

FORT RENO 🎥

Ever since it was commissioned by the US government in 1874, Fort Reno has served as a witness to the state of Oklahoma's unfolding history. It has been a US Cavalry post—the famed Ninth Cavalry of Buffalo Soldiers was stationed here—a POW camp for captured German and Italian soldiers during World War II—the prisoners built the fort's chapel—and a US Department of Agriculture research center that worked to advance farming in the state of Oklahoma, which today leads the country in rye and winter wheat production. Amelia Earhart flew her autogiro (grandfather of the helicopter) onto the airstrip in the 1920s; humorist, actor, and author Will Rogers enjoyed watching horse races here; Black Jack, the riderless ceremonial horse used in the funeral processions of Presidents Hoover, Kennedy, and Johnson, and General MacArthur, was raised and trained here. . . . So much history unfolded here, at historic Fort Reno.

The same year that Fort Reno opened its doors as a military post in charge of protecting and policing the surrounding Oklahoma Territory, George Custer and his expedition claimed to have found gold in the Black Hills, leading to a gold rush. Native Americans, falsely promised the protection of their sacred lands, began their long battle against being confined to reservations. The army forcibly resettled many Cheyenne to an area directly near the fort; three hundred managed to escape back to their ancestral lands. The fort oversaw the transformation of the surrounding Oklahoma Territory into farm and ranch lands as land rushes brought new settlers by the thousands.

The fort's location along Route 66 made it the ideal location for a military prisoner-of-war camp during World War II, as defense-related traffic kept America's byway humming with activity. More than 1,300 German soldiers, mostly captured in North Africa, were sent to Fort Reno, where they labored mainly in agriculture. Seventy prisoners were interred in the fort's cemetery.

Today you can visit 25 of the fort's buildings as well as its cemetery. The best time to visit is by the light of a lantern during one of the fort's popular ghost tours: You'll hear the stories of the restless spirits of the old post and visit with paranormal research

teams who have conducted extensive investigations to uncover the fort's long, murky history.

7107 W. Cheyenne St., El Reno, OK; (405) 262-3987; fortreno.org

JIGG'S SMOKEHOUSE

The State of Oklahoma and barbecue have a long-running friendship. Native Americans, forced to migrate to the Oklahoma Territory during the Trail of Tears, shared their whole-hog barbecue tradition. Post–Civil War cattle drives and the establishment of ranches brought meat to the table. At Governor Jack Walton's official inauguration in 1923, more than 1 mile of barbecue trenches greeted the attendees.

Jiggs is the best smokehouse along Route 66, serving up delectable barbecue since the 1970s, when local Jiggs Butchlett built it as an outlet for fresh whole turkeys and eggs from his bountiful farmlands. In 1978, a new owner with a new concept stepped in: George Klaassen transformed the meat shop into a smokehouse, serving up a whopping two menu items: ham sandwich and turkey sandwich. The only available condiment: butter.

Over time more menu items were added, and before long, it became known as the best smokehouse in the state. Today, George's son runs the show.

Foodie ▰▾ Find

JIGGS'S TRIPLE PIGSICKLE SANDWICH

This over-the-top smokehouse sandwich consists of two mesquite-smoked boneless pork rib patties layered with cheddar cheese, mayo, mustard, and a generous pour of barbecue sauce.

Plan on loosening your belt a few notches after indulging in the specialty sandwiches: The Wooly Burger packs 31 ounces of hickory-smoked ham and seven slices of summer sausage plus cheddar cheese, chow chow relish, mayonnaise, and Jiggs's very own barbecue sauce, which the establishment claims is "good enough to drink out of the bottle!" The so-called pigsickle consists of two mesquite-smoked boneless pork rib patties layered with cheddar cheese, mayo, mustard, and a generous pour of barbecue sauce; the triple pigsickle is for the tried, true, and hungry barbecue connoisseur with its extra dose of meat and cheese.

The house-made beef jerky is the ideal road-trip snack: take one bite of these hickory-smoked and marinated delights and you'll soon discover why the term "Jiggs jerk junkies" was coined. Barbecue sauce is also available by the case.

22203 N. Frontage Rd., Clinton, OK; (580) 323-5641; jiggssmokehouse.com

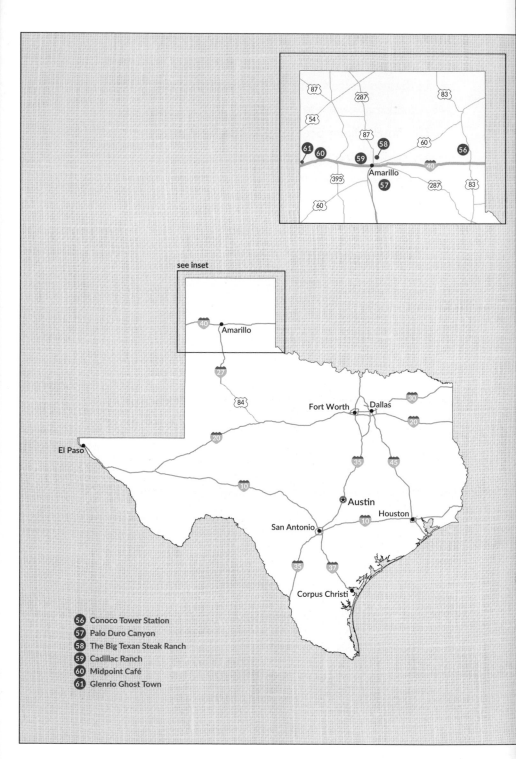

TEXAS

see inset

87
287
83
54
87
58
60
56
61 60
59
Amarillo
395
60
57
287
83
40

40
Amarillo

27

84
30
Fort Worth   Dallas
20
El Paso
20
35   45
10
★ Austin
10   Houston
San Antonio
35   37
Corpus Christi

56 Conoco Tower Station
57 Palo Duro Canyon
58 The Big Texan Steak Ranch
59 Cadillac Ranch
60 Midpoint Café
61 Glenrio Ghost Town

CONOCO TOWER STATION 📷

The Conoco Tower Station traded dingy service station ambience for Art Deco elegance. Rising like a beacon of hope for cars running low on gas, the station's four-sided obelisk spire, topped with a metal tulip, still spells out its main product, C-O-N-O-C-O fuel. While the pink-and-green service station with its adjacent U-Drop Inn Café has been repurposed into a visitor center and gift shop, you can still fill 'er up with nostalgia at this Route 66 icon.

Less than 100 years after army officer and explorer Captain R. B. Marcy crossed through the area on his way to Santa Fe, describing it as ". . . a vast, illimitable expanse of desert prairie . . .," the station was a major investment in the future of tiny Shamrock, Texas. It cost $23,000 to build, a whopping figure at the time. At night it turned on its jewels: green-and-red neon lights that could be seen from miles down Route 66 in the darkness. The U-Drop Inn Café served up premium diner fare. An in-house "Auto Laundry" washed and polished incoming automobiles. The local newspaper declared it "the swankiest of swank eating places" and "the most up-to-date edifice of its kind on US Highway 66 between Oklahoma City and Amarillo."

Today, the City of Shamrock owns the building, which has been meticulously restored back to its original appearance. It's also been modernized: You can find several supercharger power stations to fire up your Tesla. Pay a visit after sunset, when the neon glow of the Conoco Tower Station is especially sublime.

1242 N. Main St., Shamrock, TX; (806) 256-2501

PALO DURO CANYON 📷 👟

Welcome to a world of wonder, where four bioregions and countless cultures have collided over the centuries, where unique flora and fauna and majestic beauty await those brave enough to take a hike. It took thousands upon thousands of years—and a little help from the Prairie Dog Town Fork Red River—to carve out the caves, fairy-tale hoodoos, gorgeous multicolored layers of rock, and steep mesa walls of the so-called Grand Canyon of Texas. Palo Duro—"hard wood" in Spanish—Canyon, located in the heart of the Texas Panhandle, is the second largest canyon in the US. With an average width of 6 miles and a maximum depth of 1,000 feet, the canyon is decorated with trees (mesquite, red berry juniper, cottonwood, willow, and western soapberry) and wildflowers (Indian blanket, blackfoot daisy, sand sage, and prickly pear cactus). Painter Georgia O'Keeffe, who featured Palo Duro in several of her paintings, remarked, "It is a burning, seething cauldron, filled with dramatic light and color."

While most of the canyon was formed during the human-free Permian and Triassic ages, there is evidence that humans settled in the area as far back as 15,000 years ago, likely attracted by the bountiful wild game and caves that provided sustenance and shelter. In 1541, the Coronado expedition chanced upon the canyon while searching for the mythical Seven Cities of Gold. Native Americans called the canyon home until 1874, when they were forcibly removed to reservations. Several species can be found among the canyon's many hidden corners, including bobcats, coyotes, deer, roadrunners, wild turkeys, and even the rare and endangered Texas horned lizard.

The best way to experience the canyon is by foot, mountain bike, or horse thanks to more than 30 miles of hiking, biking, and equestrian trails, but you can also explore by car. The Visitor Center, located on the canyon rim, offers spectacular views. Consider camping here, too, so you can wake up to the most awe-inspiring sunrise in Texas; choose from glamping-style campsites or nestle in one of the three cabins on the canyon's rim or four limited-service cabins on the canyon floor, or be daring and check into one of the primitive drive-up sites, equestrian sites, or backpack camping areas.

Though you'll likely find them peacefully sunbathing or sleeping under a blanket of sand, beware of the Texas horned lizard: They possess a superhero-like defense mechanism that allows them to squirt an aimed stream of blood from the corners of their eyes—for a distance up to 5 feet—if they feel threatened.

11450 State Hwy. Park Rd. 5, Canyon, TX; (806) 488-2227; tpwd.texas.gov/state-parks/palo-duro-canyon

THE BIG TEXAN STEAK RANCH 🍽️ 🛏️

If you're the proud owner of a Texas-sized appetite, keep your eyes peeled for the big cow statue advertising a "free" 72-ounce steak on Interstate 40. You're approaching the Big Texan Steak Ranch, home of the mega steak, a.k.a. The Texas King. This supersize steak is free to anyone who manages to down all 4.5 pounds of steak *and* the accompanying sides in one hour or less.

R. J. "Bob" Lee opened the Big Texan Steak Ranch along Route 66 back in 1960. To drum up business, he drew up his steak deal of the century. A sign featuring a cowboy with a 10-gallon hat, gun at the ready in his holster, lets guests know that they've finally arrived.

It's hard to believe but close to 10,000 people have accomplished this foodie feat through the years. Competitive eater Molly Schuyler—who managed to down the entire meal in four minutes eighteen seconds—is the current Texan King record holder. You'll have to pay for your meal in advance—your money will be refunded if you beat the odds—and competitors are required to sit on a raised platform in the middle of the main dining room. Celebrate your Texas King Challenge win by jumping into the over-the-top Texas-shape swimming pool at the adjacent Big Texan Motel.

The 54-unit Big Texan Motel was built to resemble a main street in an old Wild West town, albeit with a more colorful palette and a late 1800s via the 1970s vibe. Traveling

Foodie Find

THE TEXAS KING AT THE BIG TEXAN STEAK RANCH

This is the king of all steak dinners! The Texas King mega steak is free to anyone who manages to down all 72 ounces—plus the accompanying shrimp cocktail, baked potato, salad, and a roll with butter—in one hour or less.

with your favorite horse? Twenty Texas-size horse stalls, a 60-foot round pen, and four gated runs give equine guests the chance to stretch their legs in a safe, secure stable. Be sure to stop at the ranch's unique gift shop and say hello to the resident rattlesnake.

"The spirit of Route 66 was all about hundreds of independent roadside business 'entrepreneurs' presenting their local cultures and beliefs to the passing travelers," shares second-generation owner Bobby Lee. "These STOPS made the journey as much

fun as the destination. When the new superhighways bypassed the Mother Road, corporations began littering roads with their pad-site wastelands, cluttered with 'cookie cutter' style of chain motels/restaurants. Over the past 55 years, the Big

Texan has always held true to its roots and to our responsibility in keeping FUN in the Great American Road Trip. We love what we're doing and our guests (past-present-future) recognize and embrace it."

7701 E. Interstate 40, Amarillo, TX; (806) 372-6000; bigtexan.com

CADILLAC RANCH

Ten miles southwest of Amarillo, Texas, along the old alignment of Route 66, 10 Cadillacs—half-buried, nose-first—rise from the earth of a picturesque cow pasture. Born between 1949 and 1963 and rescued from a junkyard eternity, this uniquely American monument celebrates the life—and death—of the luxury Cadillac.

Chip Lord, Doug Michels, and Hudson Marquez, members of the avant-garde art collective Ant Farm, are responsible for this unofficial tribute to the golden age of the

Wikimedia Commons

automobile. In a 2016 *Amarillo Globe-News* article, Marquez explained the inspiration behind the noteworthy addition to middle-of-nowhere Amarillo: "Chip and I were living in the mountains north of San Francisco, and there was a book meant for kids left in a bar near where we lived. . . . It was called *The Look of Cars*, and there was something on the rise and fall of the tail fin." (Note that as you walk along the row of buried Caddies the tailfin slowly works its way out of the newer models and into history.) "I've always loved the Cadillacs," explained Marquez. "The spirit of Cadillac Ranch is 'Welcome, look at this, isn't this fun?'"

But the Ant Farm needed money to get their Cadillac-size idea off the ground. They researched eccentric millionaires who might be willing to fund an outrageous art project and successfully zeroed in on an Amarillo-based businessman and philanthropist named Stanley Marsh 3. (Marsh considered the Roman numeral "III" to be pretentious and preferred the suffix "3.") In 1974, they buried the once-regal Caddies at an angle corresponding to that of the Great Pyramid of Giza.

The Cadillacs once wore their original snazzy paint jobs but have changed their look over time. They lost their windows, radios, speakers, and a few other parts to vandals. Visitors are welcome to paint the cars and ply them with graffiti, making every visit to this iconic American masterpiece unique.

Cadillac Ranch is on I-40 (formerly Route 66), just west of the Amarillo city line. Take exit 60 and follow the frontage road on the south side of I-40 east for about one mile. Park your car along the shoulder. Open sunrise to sunset; admission is always free.

MIDPOINT CAFÉ ⊙

Pull up to the Midpoint Café in tiny Adrian, Texas, and give yourself a pat on the back as you park. You've reached the geo-mathematical midpoint of Route 66, exactly 1,139 miles from Chicago and 1,139 miles to Los Angeles. It's no surprise that this iconic café's slogan is "when you're here, you're halfway there."

You might already recognize Midpoint Café: It starred as Flo's V-8 Café in the 2006 animated film *Cars*. Three of the movie's most memorable characters, Flo, Mia, and Tia, were based on former owner Fran Houser and two waitresses.

Built in 1928, the diner came into its own when Route 66 reached its bubbling point in the 1940s. Omelets, hotcakes, burgers, fries, and, of course, the café's so-called "Ugly Crust" pies, were served up to satisfied customers 24 hours a day, 365 days a year.

Joann Harwell, Midpoint Café's pastry chef, came up with the ugly crust pie concept after noting that the pies she baked up, following her grandmother's recipe, recreated the taste but not the beautiful crust she remembered. Don't mind the messy crusts. Midpoint's pies—available in pecan, chocolate chip, apple, lemon meringue, and chocolate, on a rotating basis—are so delicious you'll want to grab a slice (or an entire pie) for the road ahead.

When Interstate 40 opened its doors for business in 1969, bypassing Adrian, business declined. But the memorable Midpoint Café retains the flavors of a bygone era and remains an iconic stopping point for Mother Road travelers. The adjacent, retro filling station has been transformed into a gift shop and the Fabulous 40 Motel, circa 1967, recently reopened after a decade of decline. The café is no longer open 24/7, but it's usually packed with customers from around the world.

305 W. Historic Route 66, Adrian, TX; (806) 538-6379

Foodie ☕ Find

UGLY CRUST PIES AT MIDPOINT CAFÉ

Grab a slice (or two) of Midpoint's Ugly Crust pies—availabie in pecan, chocolate chip, apple, lemon meringue, and chocolate, on a rotating basis.

GLENRIO GHOST TOWN 📷

On the high desert plains connecting Texas and New Mexico lies a town inhabited by only the ghosts of the past. Once upon a time its diners, saloons, motels, filling stations, and dance hall burst with locals and outsiders who breezed into town via Route 66. Today, you'll be lucky if you encounter a rolling tumbleweed. Though it once burned bright, Glenrio blew out like a neon lightbulb.

Glenrio popped up as a railroad stop in 1906 when the tracks of the Chicago, Rock Island, and Gulf Railways were extended west of Amarillo. Located along the state lines, part of the town sits in Texas and the other, New Mexico. In 1913, the Ozark Trails, the multistate highway system that predated Route 66, was routed through Glenrio. In 1926, it morphed into Route 66, and the town was witness to a flash of prosperity. Gas stations, a diner, and a motel sprouted on the north side of the highway; to the south, a Welcome to Texas station greeted guests with a precious commodity, water, for drinking and cooling off overheated engines, a common automotive issue in the early days of Route 66. Life in Glenrio came to a screeching halt in the 1970s when Interstate

40 bypassed the town. In mere months, it morphed into a town inhabited only by the ghosts of days gone by.

Most of the buildings are now lost to the desert sands of time, but about 17 remain, though they're mostly covered with debris, missing windows, and overgrown with weeds, including two Art Moderne–influenced beauties: a Texaco gas station and the nearby diner. You can also walk along the original Route 66 roadbed.

See if you can spot the former watering hole, the State Line Bar: It's situated on the New Mexico side of Glenrio, since the Texas side was part of then-dry Deaf Smith County.

Glenrio, TX

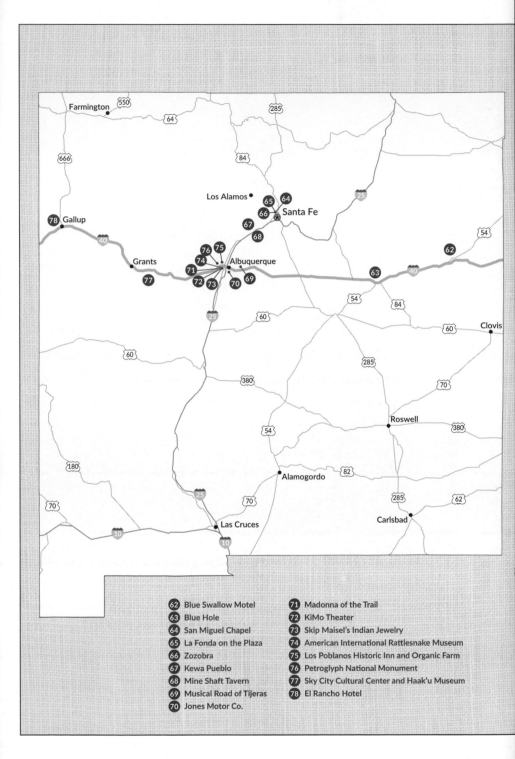

NEW MEXICO

62 Blue Swallow Motel
63 Blue Hole
64 San Miguel Chapel
65 La Fonda on the Plaza
66 Zozobra
67 Kewa Pueblo
68 Mine Shaft Tavern
69 Musical Road of Tijeras
70 Jones Motor Co.

71 Madonna of the Trail
72 KiMo Theater
73 Skip Maisel's Indian Jewelry
74 American International Rattlesnake Museum
75 Los Poblanos Historic Inn and Organic Farm
76 Petroglyph National Monument
77 Sky City Cultural Center and Haak'u Museum
78 El Rancho Hotel

BLUE SWALLOW MOTEL ☁

Rambling along Route 66, the neon sign of Blue Swallow Court, advertising TV and 100 percent Refrigerated Air—hard-to-find amenities long ago—once attracted travelers like moths to a flame. Tourist town Tucumcari lays claim to 5 miles of Route 66, where the spirit of the Mother Road remains fully intact.

The 12-unit, L-shape, pink-stucco Blue Swallow opened in 1939. Built by local carpenter W. A. Huggins and run by eastern New Mexico rancher Ted Jones and his wife, the Blue Swallow originally offered only 10 rooms along with an on-site café. Two more units were added in the early 1950s, along with a central office and manager's residence. Garage units, located between the sleeping units, made the motel the ideal

New Mexico Department of Tourism

LILLIAN REDMAN'S BLUE SWALLOW BENEDICTION

Greetings Traveler:

In ancient times, there was a prayer for "The Stranger Within Our Gates." Because this motel is a human institution to serve people, and not solely a money-making organization, we hope that God will grant you peace and rest while you are under our roof.

May this room and motel be your "second" home. May those you love be near you in thoughts and dreams. Even though we may not get to know you, we hope that you will be as comfortable and happy as if you were in your own house.

May the business that brought you this way prosper. May every call you make and every message you receive add to your joy. When you leave, may your journey be safe.

We are all travelers. From "birth till death," we travel between the eternities. May these days be pleasant for you, profitable for society, helpful for those you meet, and a joy to those you know and love best.

Sincerely yours,
Lillian Redman
(owner of the Blue Swallow Motel from 1958-98)

drive-in/drive-out motel for motorists hoping to travel the length of the route in record time.

In the late 1950s, Floyd Redman purchased the motel as an engagement gift for his future bride, Lillian. The kind couple soon became Route 66 legends, adored for accepting items for barter instead of cash on occasion, a gift to cash-poor travelers in a bind. Ms. Redman had once been a traveler to Tucumcari herself when her family journeyed from the east via covered wagon in 1915. She summed up the spirit of the Blue Swallow when she said, "I end up traveling the highway in my heart with whoever stops here for the night." Indeed, she would run the hotel long after her husband's death and into her late eighties.

Like so many other small towns, Tucumcari lost the Route 66 traffic it relied too heavily upon to today's Interstate 40. In the late 1990s, new owners stepped in, restoring it to its former glory. The dim blue neon swallow sign glowed brightly once again, a good old-fashioned rotary-dial phone system was reinstalled, and the original fixtures and 1950s Albuquerque furniture were refurbished along with the rooms themselves.

You might recognize Tucumcari from old episodes of *Rawhide* (1959–66), starring Clint Eastwood, which was shot in part here, while the Cozy Cone Motel of Pixar's 2006 hit *Cars* was inspired by the Blue Swallow. The original car garages with their original wooden doors still stand adjacent to their assigned rooms, perfect for motorcycles and vintage cars. Depart in the early evening so you have a chance to drive into the glorious New Mexico sunset on what was once the main street of America.

Lillian Redman provided each guest a copy of the blessing on page 133, still given to travelers passing through the Blue Swallow Motel today.

815 E. Route 66 Blvd., Tucumcari, NM; (575) 461-9849; blueswallowmotel.com

BLUE HOLE 🥽

It's one of the most popular scuba diving destinations in the US, located in the arid, landlocked state of New Mexico, along old Route 66.

Wait . . . what?! Scuba diving in a tiny desert town??

The Blue Hole of Santa Rosa is the shining jewel of Route 66, a giant, hourglass-shape, 80-foot-diameter swimming hole formed thousands of years ago, here, in the middle of the high desert. Just imagine what it must have been like for early motorists traveling along Route 66 as they came across this mirage of swimming hole after miles of driving through dry, sand-swept vistas.

Though it appears to be a swimming pool sent from above, the Blue Hole is officially a spring-fed sinkhole, formed thousands of years ago by water erosion and seepage. With 3,000 gallons of water flowing per minute, the water is crystal clear, so even if you're at its center you can spot its craggy limestone walls and scuba divers, making their way downward, far beneath your flippers.

You can always jump into its glistening, deep-blue waters and enjoy the cool, constant 64-degree Fahrenheit temperature, but the only way to reach the bottom is via scuba diving: the Blue Hole's diameter expands to 130 feet at its bottom, which lies

almost 80 feet below the desert surface. A labyrinth of elaborate caverns, with access points throughout the sinkhole, is dangerous and seldom explored.

Scuba divers will appreciate the incredible visibility, but descending to the depths is a challenge. Since Santa Rosa stands at an elevation of 4,616 feet, divers need to use high-altitude dive tables. The narrow cavern passageways have trapped and swallowed up even the most experienced divers over the years.

Located just off old Route 66, the Blue Hole is open 24/7 for swimmers. Divers will need a permit, sold at the on-site scuba shop along with rental equipment.

Route 66, Santa Rosa, NM; (575) 472-3763; santarosabluehole.com

SAN MIGUEL CHAPEL 🔟

It's the most poignant place of worship near the old alignment of Route 66, which once cut through the heart of Santa Fe, and the oldest church in the United States. With a history that reaches back to the early 1600s, the San Miguel Chapel was built as the "Hermita de San Miguel," replacing a *kiva*, a spiritual center used by the Tlaxcalan peoples for religious rituals and political meetings. Franciscan friars oversaw the construction of this important gathering place, part of their mission to serve a small congregation of soldiers, laborers, and Native Americans of the Barrio de Analco, a historic neighborhood located on the south side of the Santa Fe River, sometime between 1610 and 1626.

Over the centuries, the humble adobe San Miguel Chapel has seen it all. It witnessed the Pueblo Revolt of 1680 when the indigenous Pueblo people took a brave stand against the Spanish colonizers; by the early 1700s, it was a place of worship exclusively for Spanish soldiers. In 1872, a severe storm followed by an earthquake toppled the top two tiers of its bell tower. Not all the tiers were replaced, but the bell, cast in Spain in 1356, survived the fall and proudly rings to this day. Some worshipers never left the chapel: Excavations in the 1950s revealed human remains, buried underneath the original dirt floor.

The altar fittingly commands the attention of visitors, with its wooden altar screen, or *reredos*. An inscription on the lower left-hand corner reads "This altar was erected through the piety of Don José Antonio Ortis in the year 1798." At its center stands a statue of San Miguel, likely carved in old Mexico around 1700. Two paintings depicting the Annunciation, believed to be the work of one of the disciples of the great 17th-century Spanish Baroque painter Bartolomé Esteban Murillo, flank the altar.

Two paintings on animal hides, located on either wall of the nave, are of particular interest: One buffalo hide depicts Christ on the Cross; the other, a deerskin, showcases St. John the Baptist. The Franciscan Friars who painted these hides in about 1630 used them as teaching aids that they could easily roll up and carry around as they worked to convert the Pueblo peoples to Christianity.

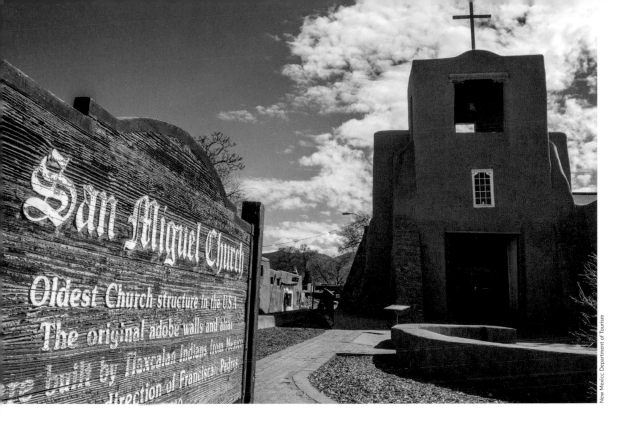

One of the best ways to experience the San Miguel Chapel is to attend Latin mass—offered at 2 p.m. on Sunday—within its walls. The *Schola Cantorum of Santa Fe* sings Vespers and Gregorian chants every third Sunday of the month at 4 p.m.

401 Old Santa Fe Trail, Santa Fe, NM; (505) 983-3974; sanmiguelchapel.org

LA FONDA ON THE PLAZA 🍽

Lined with hallowed, historic monuments (including the Palace of the Governors, the New Mexico Museum of Art, and the Cathedral Basilica of Saint Francis of Assisi), and centered by a picture-perfect park, Santa Fe Plaza has been the beating heart of the city since the early 1600s, when it served as a fort that enclosed a prison, barracks, a chapel, and even the governor's residence. Long before Route 66 rolled into town, this scenic plaza was the terminus for the 800-mile-long Old Santa Fe Trail, a transportation route

pioneered by the Spaniards at the end of the 18th century, linking the Southwestern city to Independence, Missouri.

Built on the site of a former *fonda*, or inn, the Pueblo Revival La Fonda on the Plaza advertised itself as "the purest Santa Fe type of architecture and one of the most truly distinctive hotels anywhere between Chicago and San Diego" when it opened in 1922. Soldiers, gold seekers, gamblers, politicians, trappers, and tourists from near and far called La Fonda home when in town. It soon became *the* place to see and been seen, as journalist Ernie Pyle noted, "You could go there any time of day and see a few artists in the bar . . . a goateed gentleman from Austria or a maharajah from India or a New York broker. . . . You never met anyone anywhere except at La Fonda."

Snapped up by the Santa Fe Railway in 1925, it became a Harvey Company hotel one year later. The Harvey company connection brought tourists in by the trainload, thanks to its innovative cultural tours of the scenic Southwest. Harvey also brought in young women from across the country to work here as waitresses and maids, in exchange for a generous stipend, room and board, and the opportunity to travel and experience a glimpse of independence, an adventure memorialized in the 1946 MGM musical film *The Harvey Girls*, starring Judy Garland.

Today, La Fonda on the Plaza is a vibrant luxury hotel that offers a chance to experience Santa Fe as it was in the roaring twenties, when the Southwest was just opening its doors to tourism. The original design elements remain in place—exposed *vigas* (ceiling beams), colorful Mexican tiles, stained glass skylights, hammered tin chandeliers—adding to the overall air of a Southwestern romance.

Soak up as much old-world charm as you can by spending the night at this history-filled inn, or at least enjoy a meal at the La Plazuela, the in-hotel restaurant featuring classic New Mexican cuisine in a sunlit setting. The hotel also offers a complimentary, docent-led art and history tour of the hotel, which is filled with stories about the iconic Harvey girls, the stunning Southwest architecture, and the world-class art collection that graces every nook and cranny.

100 E. San Francisco St., Santa Fe, NM; (505) 982-5511; lafondasantafe.com

ZOZOBRA 📷

Fifty-foot-tall Zozobra is Santa Fe's number-one most wanted marionette, charged with robbing unsuspecting citizens of their hopes and dreams and filling their hearts with doom and gloom. He takes up residence every September in Santa Fe's Fort Marcy Park only to be burned at the stake.

Zozobra, a.k.a. Old Man Gloom, was born in 1924, in the backyard of Will Shuster, a quintessentially free-spirited Santa Fe artist. He isn't your standard, happy-faced marionette, either. His skin and bones are made of muslin and wood, his insides stuffed with shredded paper. Part ghost, part monster, and inspired by the Holy Week celebrations

of the Yaqui Indians, Shuster fashioned him after Judas. His name, Zozobra, translates to anxiety in Spanish, adding to the misery he signifies.

Every autumn, he's tricked into coming out of hiding with an invitation to historic Fort Marcy Park to take part in the annual Fiestas de Santa Fe, which mark the anniversary of the 1692 reconquest of New Mexico. Legend has it that Zozobra hatches an annual plan: to cast an evil spell over the children of Santa Fe and rob them of their happiness. Thank God for the Fire Spirit, who arrives on the scene with a torch and sets Zozobra ablaze. As Zozobra burns under the starry sky, so too do the worries and troubles of Santa Fe's fine citizens . . . and visiting tourists.

If you can't make the annual celebration, write down your worry on a slip of paper and leave it in the "gloom box" found in the offices of the *Santa Fe Reporter* at 132 E. Marcy St. in the weeks leading up to the burn: All the written-down worries in the gloom box will be placed at Zozobra's feet and fed to the flames of time along with Zozobra himself.

The Burning of Zozobra takes place on the Friday before Labor Day, rain or shine, at 9:30 p.m. in Fort Marcy Park, 490 Bishops Lodge Rd., Santa Fe, NM.

KEWA PUEBLO 📷 🖼️

The Kewa people are well known for their fine arts and crafts: They not only reflect their most cherished traditions but also the surrounding nature that sustains their traditional

way of life. Residents here have somehow managed to hold tight to religious and cultural practices, despite Spanish colonialism and the routing of the railroad and Route 66, which ran through the area from 1926 to 1932.

The Kewa have been crafting fine jewelry and *heishi*, colorful beads, out of the rich turquoise stones of the nearby, ancient Cerrillos mines for centuries. Throughout the pueblo, roadside stands offer some of the most stunning jewelry, silverwork, and pottery that you'll encounter as you journey along Route 66, making for a wonderful opportunity to talk directly with the artisans behind the beautiful wares.

The historic pueblo was previously known as the Pueblo of Santo Domingo, until its tribal council unanimously voted to return to the original name, Kewa (Khe-wa), in the native Keresan language. The Spanish arrived here in the late 1500s, eventually claiming Santo Domingo as a provincial capital. Uprisings and flooding threatened to destroy the pueblo forever. But today the old pueblo is on the National Register of Historic Places and remains the vibrant home of more than 3,600 tribal members.

Take a moment to explore the plazas and the Spanish mission–style church located on the edge of the pueblo. The roadside stands, which popped up alongside Route 66 in its heyday, serve as mini-museums, while also offering motorists a wide array of quality, locally made pueblo jewelry, pottery, and other crafts. The best time to visit the pueblo is on Labor Day weekend, when almost 400 Native American artists from across the US convene here for the annual Santo Domingo Arts and Crafts Market.

The town's popular, two-story trading post, erected in 1881, is one of the oldest along Route 66 and was recently restored after a devastating fire. While it once sold kitschy souvenirs, today the trading post serves as an arts incubator and a place for the tribe's artisans to showcase their finest works of art.

The Kewa Pueblo (formerly the Santo Domingo Pueblo) lies on the original 1926 alignment of Route 66, approximately 35 miles north of Albuquerque and 25 miles south of Santa Fe, NM, via the Santo Domingo exit on Interstate 25.

MINE SHAFT TAVERN 📷

Tiny Madrid, New Mexico's mines opened for business hundreds of years ago, when indigenous inhabitants began to search for turquoise and lead deposits in the nearby hills. The Spaniards arrived in 1540, hoping for gold but settling for silver. In 1835, coal was discovered, but large-scale mining didn't take off until the 1880s, when the Santa Fe Railroad swept into town. By the early 1900s, the town's 30 square miles of mines were company owned. The 3,000-plus residents lived in company-provided homes, walked upon company-paved streets, and shopped at company-owned stores; they drank here at the company-owned tavern, their wages funneled right back into the company owner's pockets.

The original Mine Shaft Tavern was built circa 1895. Then it burned down, on Christmas Day, 1944. By 1947 the current Mine Shaft Tavern rose from the ashes. Thirsty miners enjoyed many a cold drink, standing up at the tall bar, made of a 40-foot-long pine pole, after having spent their entire working day hunched over in the dark depths of the mine.

Wikimedia Commons/Rvaldez4108

Bloody Mary, Bloody Mary . . .
Rumor has it that the Mine Shaft Tavern is haunted by those who never made it out of the nearby shaft. Orbs often appear in photos taken here, so grab a handcrafted Bloody Mary and snap a few selfies to see if you've attracted any ghosts. If you're feeling brave, visit the restroom where several patrons have reported seeing another face staring over their shoulders, in the reflection of the mirror.

By the 1950s, however, natural gas was fueling America, and Madrid's coal mines closed forever. For about 20 years, the town was truly a ghost town. Then in the 1970s, artists moved in, taking over the empty homes and businesses. Once again, the long bar at the Mineshaft Tavern was packed with patrons. Take a look at the paintings above the tavern's bar, which capture Madrid's journey from boomtown to ghost town and back again.

2846 NM-14, Madrid, NM; (505) 473-0743; themineshafttavern.com

MUSICAL ROAD OF TIJERAS 👟

It's the most musical segment of Route 66. Drive along this quarter-mile stretch in tiny Tijeras, New Mexico, and the road will play you a tune. If you tend to put your pedal to the metal, you'll miss the music: The song, "America the Beautiful," only plays for those that follow the rules of the road, namely the 45-mile-per-hour speed limit.

In 2014, National Geographic and the New Mexico Department of Transportation installed musical rumble strips, perfectly positioned grooves that create different pitches are you drive along the road, playing the song via the vibrations in your car's wheels. Matt Kennicot, director of communications for NMDOT, explained the phenomenon

John Phelan

best: "Anything that vibrates 330 times per second will produce an E note. This applies to violin strings and car tires alike. So all you need to do to produce an E note is make sure that the car hits 330 strips in one second at 45 miles per hour, a scenario that works out to each rumble strip being placed 2.4 inches apart."

The roadway was selected for this noteworthy update in part for its beauty but also because too many cars were zooming through town at top speeds. The Musical Road of Tijeras is a musical reminder that it's best to slow down and enjoy the ride.

The Musical Road of Tijeras is labeled as eastbound Route 333 (formerly Route 66) and is located between mile markers 4 and 5, near exit 170 in Tijeras, New Mexico.

JONES MOTOR COMPANY 🍽

US Route 66 arrived in Albuquerque in 1937, forever changing the landscape of Central Avenue, which soon began to buzz with automobiles. In 1930, there were only six buildings standing on this 18-mile stretch of road in the quirky Nob Hill neighborhood; by 1939, a whopping 44 buildings housed businesses built to make a buck off incoming

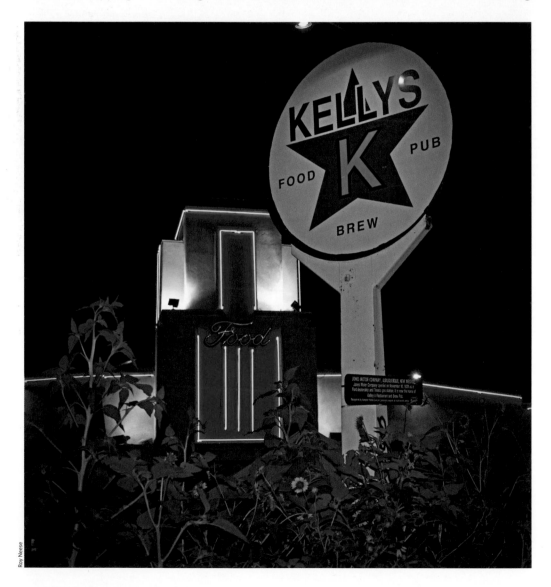

Roy Neese

Roy Neese

motorists. One of these buildings was the Jones Motor Company, an Art Moderne gem of a service station where patrons could also trade their jalopy in for the latest model.

When it opened in 1939, the Jones Motor Company was the most modern service station along the Mother Road. The one-story, white stucco building with its stepped tower and neon ornamentation, typical of the Streamline Moderne style, had two Texaco gas pumps in front and a large display window that showcased shiny new Fords. Salesmen were on hand, ready to make a sale. Most early Route 66 motorists could only dream of owning a fancy new car and stopped here to repair their flat tires, a common problem due to cars overloaded with the humble possessions of families making their way westward.

Ralph Jones, the man behind the business, was not only a prosperous local businessman but also the president of the local Route 66 Association, which must have given him a little insight into the prosperity that lay down the road.

Today, high desert craft brews replace cars in this retro building. The Jones Motor Company moved on in 1957; Kellys Brew Pub now serves up appetizers, wraps, burgers, sandwiches, and award-winning beers, all brewed on site, to the hip patrons who populate the large patio arranged around the old pumps and alight with the soft glow of neon.

3222 Central Ave. SE; Albuquerque, NM; (505) 262-2739; kellysbrewpub.com

MADONNA OF THE TRAIL ⊙

She's a lady you wouldn't want to mess with. She holds her baby tightly in one arm, yet another kid tugs at her long prairie skirt. Bonnet tied, protected from the hard-beating sun, she looks westward, rifle at the ready. At 18 feet tall with a weight of a whopping 5 tons, she's lean and mean, stone-faced. She's made of stone, too—pink Missouri granite and marble, lead ore, and cement. It's fitting that this beautiful, bold Madonna, so strong, so obviously determined and unsinkable, stands as a symbol of the indomitable spirit of the many women who made the challenging journey west.

The Madonna on the Trail has 11 sisters, standing at 11 other points of the National Old Trails Road, a precursor to Route 66 that stretched from Baltimore to Los Angeles, formed upon the even older National Road and Santa Fe Trail. They were all part of a project dreamed up by the National Society of Daughters of the American Revolution, to honor the pioneering women who built the West. Built in the late 1920s, they were created by August Leimbach, a German-American sculptor who worked out of St. Louis. The sites were chosen under the guidance of the president of the National Old Trails Road Association, a Missouri judge named Harry S. Truman. At the dedication of the statue located in Springfield, Ohio, Truman remarked:

"They [the women] were just as brave or braver than their men because, in many cases, they went with sad hearts and trembling bodies. They went, however, and

endured every hardship that befalls a pioneer." Years later, Truman would serve as our nation's 33rd president.

Albuquerque's Madonna of the Trail arrived via a grand parade from downtown to this small square on the grounds of the Federal Courthouse. She gazed upon the next generation of pioneers making their way west along Route 66 from 1928 until 1937, when the Route was aligned onto Central Avenue.

Marble Avenue and Fourth Street, Albuquerque, NM

KIMO THEATER 👟 📷

Albuquerque's iconic KiMo lives up to its bold name, which in the language of the nearby Isleta Pueblo translates to "King of Its Kind." It was built as a movie and vaudeville theater in 1927, the same year that *The Jazz Singer*, the first feature film presented as a talkie, hit the silver screen; one year earlier, Route 66 opened, bringing business in from out of town as motorists passed through downtown Albuquerque from north to south on what is today 4th Street.

The story behind the KiMo reflects the American dream of a humble immigrant. When Oreste Bachechi immigrated to the area from Italy in 1885, he could hardly have imagined that one day he'd be a wealthy man. His first humble business was a tent saloon near the railroad station. Bachechi dreamed of building a glitzy theater of his own, one that would pay tribute to the many Native Americans who had welcomed him to his new hometown with open arms, while also offering a chance for his neighbors to experience a taste of Hollywood in the Southwest. When he expanded into liquor sales, he found prosperity and began in earnest to make his pie in the sky a reality by hiring the renowned Kansas City, Missouri–based architectural firm the Boller Brothers, the brains behind the architecture of more than 100 movie palaces across the US.

The KiMo is the shining star of Pueblo Deco, which merged flamboyant Art Deco elements with the artistic traditions of the Native Southwest peoples into one

over-the-top design style. The three-story, sandy brown stucco theater building features just about every Native American motif you can imagine—canoes, buffalo skulls, war drums, thunderbirds, the mighty sun—while the interior went a step further and re-creates a ceremonial kiva, a spiritual space. Even the air vents were designed to appear as Navajo rugs.

Like so many other beloved gems along Route 66, the theater came close to demolition in the 1970s. The brave citizens of Albuquerque stepped in and restored it to its former glory, and the KiMO today offers a rich variety of cultural programing and entertainment of all genres. Can't catch a show? Take a docent-led tour; they're offered at least once a week so check the KiMo calendar before you pay a visit.

Be forewarned: The KiMo is home to a resident ghost, the spirit of a little boy who died here in the lobby in a horrific water heater explosion in 1951. Over the years, performers have learned that it's best to leave a little offering for the ghost, and a backstage shrine overflows with small mementos to appease the ghost and ensure a smooth show.

423 Central Ave. NW, Albuquerque, NM; (505) 768-3522; kimotickets.com

SKIP MAISEL'S INDIAN JEWELRY 📟

Maurice Maisel began his illustrious sales career peddling matches on the streets of New York at age 12. Later he became a Western Union messenger boy, earning $3.50 a week. When he was diagnosed with tuberculosis, doctors gave him just seven years to live. But Maisel refused to give up: he requested a transfer to the dry mountain air of Denver, where he worked as a telegrapher. He was soon transferred to Albuquerque, where, instead of finding himself buried 6 feet underground, his good health returned. He decided to go into business for himself, opening a curio shop at 117 South First St., in 1923. Maisel's Indian Trading Post was the most popular Indian trading post along Route 66 during its heyday. At one point, it employed as many as 300 people, mainly Native Americans, who created their beautiful jewelry, pottery, and handicrafts on-site, to the amazement of customers from far and wide. From its very beginning to today, Maisel's Indian Trading Post offers the largest selection of Indian jewelry in the Southwest.

The store itself is a grand Pueblo Revival–style masterpiece. Its colorful façade features large display windows showcasing beautiful handcrafted goods from pueblos across New Mexico, topped by murals depicting Southwestern Indians in ceremonial clothing. Bright red neon lights still attract passing motorists. Inside, the shop is packed with turquoise jewelry, the stones sourced from local mines; Pueblo pottery; Navajo rugs and sand paintings; and Hopi kachinas, small collectible figurines that represent cherished spirit-beings. Local Native Americans still create their crafts on-site, and the

inventory changes daily, as sellers are constantly popping in to unload more precious goods for sale.

Maisel died in the 1960s, and the store was sold and later closed. Then, in the 1980s Maurice Maisel's grandson, Skip, stepped in to restore and reopen the store. Today, Maurice's granddaughter, Terry Maisel Haas, lovingly keeps the legendary trading post alive and in the family.

510 Central Ave. SW, Albuquerque, NM; (505) 738-1934; skipmaisels.com

AMERICAN INTERNATIONAL RATTLESNAKE MUSEUM ◉

One of if not *the* most dangerous animal you might encounter while traveling along Route 66 is the western diamondback rattlesnake. This venomous, heavy-bodied snake, with its menacing, triangular-shaped head, can reach a length of up to 7 feet. The dark,

diamond-shape patterns along its back give it its name. It can be found in the deserts, grassy plains, forests, rocky hillsides, and areas along the coast and throughout the southwestern United States and northern half of Mexico, waiting, coiled in the shade of low-growing shrubs or rocks, for its next victim. If you hear its distinct warning signal—the western diamondback can move its rattle back and forth 60 or more times per second—freeze, assess the situation, and figure out how to slowly make your way to safety. Though bites are rare—these creatures are instinctual and would rather avoid people altogether—they can cause heavy internal bleeding, severe muscle damage, convulsions, and even death.

Albuquerque's small yet fascinating Rattlesnake Museum showcases this incredible yet often misunderstood creature, through artwork, artifacts, memorabilia, and the largest collection of live rattlesnakes in the world.

The snakes that live here might be deadly if left unsupervised though their cute names counter their menacing reputation. Groucho the Baja California rattlesnake is named for the bushy eyebrow-like markings over his large eyes; Ramona, the endangered mottled rock rattlesnake, sports a cryptic coloration to help conceal herself from predators; Beautiful Marilyn, the ultra-rare resident western diamondback, is missing her pigment, melanin, hence her ghostly appearance. These are just three of the 100 rattlesnakes, representing 34 species, that you can spend some up-close and personal time with here, minus the threat of earning a deadly bite.

Bob Myers, the museum's founder and director, created the museum with two goals in mind: to help people overcome rattlesnake fears and educate them on how rattlesnakes have influenced our lives. Though according to the New Mexico Poison Center, about 75 to 100 people are bitten by rattlesnakes in the state every year, this museum debunks the myths surrounding the serpents, highlighting their friendlier, more fascinating traits.

202 San Felipe St. NW, Albuquerque, NM; (505) 242-6569; rattlesnakes.com

LOS POBLANOS HISTORIC INN AND ORGANIC FARM

Set on 25 idyllic acres in Albuquerque, near the banks of the Rio Grande, it's easy to get lost among the fragrant lavender fields and lush gardens populated with peacocks and roadrunners at Los Poblanos, one of the most magnificent historic inns in the Southwest. Designed in 1932 by architect John Gaw Meem, the "Father of Santa Fe Style," Los Poblanos immerses guests in its stunning natural beauty and works hard to preserve its long agricultural history.

The picturesque land surrounding the inn was originally inhabited by the ancient Anasazi; later it became the site of a ranch worked by the Poblanos, settlers to the area from Pueblo, Mexico. In the 1930s, it inaugurated a model experimental farm that

housed the original Creamland Dairies, home to healthy herds of Guernsey and Holstein cows, milk suppliers to growing Albuquerque. The farm also played a role in reducing American dependence on imported sugar beets by figuring out how to best raise sugar beets in the challenging, semi-arid climate, while a greenhouse was used as a laboratory for raising new varieties of roses and chrysanthemums that would go on to conquer the commercial market.

The original experimental ranch boasted 800 acres, all owned by state congressman Albert Simms and his wife, Ruth Hanna McCormick Simms, and was the social hub for Albuquerque high society in the 1930s. Ruth was responsible for the hiring of numerous WPA artists and local craftsmen to beautify the regal adobe ranch house that today serves as the 50-room boutique-style inn.

Los Poblanos still features a model farm, though now the focus is on organic, sustainable farming, as well as the preservation of the many heirloom and native varieties grown in this region for centuries. Many of the crops here are considered endangered,

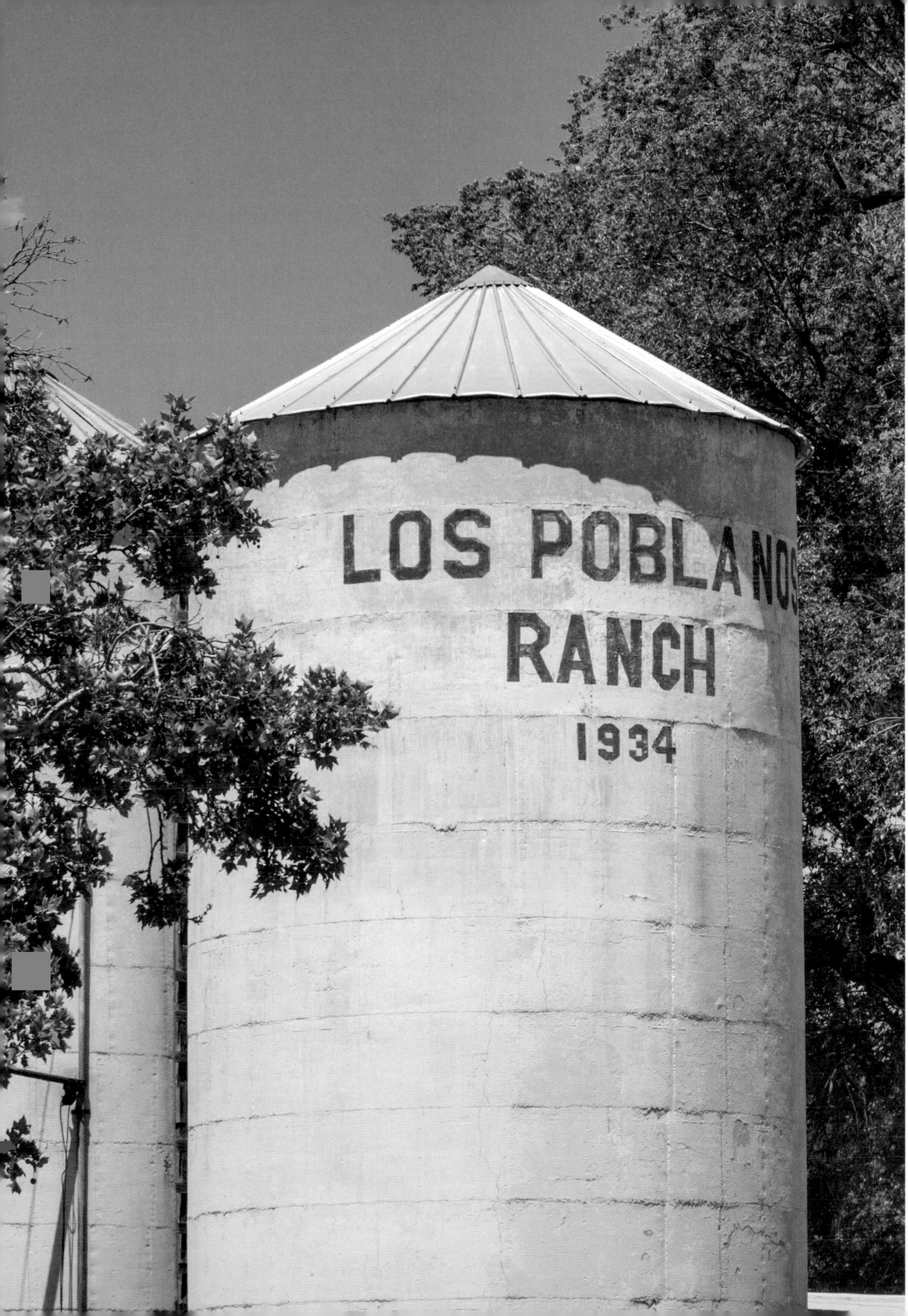

New Mexico Department of Tourism

especially the flavorful Chimayo chilies, O'odham cowpeas, casaba melons, brown tepary beans, and Magdalena big cheese squash, all of which will find their way to the table at the in-hotel Campo restaurant. While you can always enjoy a relaxing stay at the Inn, consider taking one of the many workshops or even volunteer on the farm, planting, weeding, or harvesting the organically grown produce for part of your stay.

Los Poblanos is so peaceful and relaxing, and you're bound to feel as if you've stepped back in time as you explore the bucolic grounds. Stroll the winding pebbled pathways dotted with cottonwoods, perfumed roses, and the rustic, Spanish tile fountains of the formal Rose Greely Gardens. Greely (1887–1969) was the first female licensed architect in Washington, DC, and designed more than 500 landscapes across the US in her 40-year career.

4803 Rio Grande Blvd NW; Los Ranchos De Albuquerque, NM; (505) 344-9297; lospoblanos.com

PETROGLYPH NATIONAL MONUMENT

With its five dormant volcanic cones and 17-mile basalt escarpment, the Petroglyph National Monument is unique not only in its landscape but also in its rich history, recorded on its very own rocks.

Ten thousand years ago, a series of powerful eruptions formed Albuquerque's West Mesa, which dominates the city's western horizon. Molten lava poured downhill via old waterways, called *arroyos*; over time, the lava cooled, forming basalt boulders that were later carved with spiritual motifs by the ancient, indigenous peoples of the Rio Grande Valley. This landscape of symbols is still regarded by the Western Pueblos, Navajos, and Apaches as one of the last remaining undesecrated sacred sites in the Southwest, a place where it's still possible to connect with both their ancestors and to the Spirit World beyond.

Operated and staffed by the City of Albuquerque Open Space Division, the trail system at Petroglyph National Monument will lead you to more than 100 identified petroglyphs hidden along paved pathways at four major sites. Start your journey at the visitor center, where park staff can recommend which trail will best fit your time frame and hiking ability and provide you with maps.

It is estimated that there are nearly 20,000 petroglyphs within Petroglyph National Monument and more than 20 local Native American pueblos and tribes are culturally affiliated with the monument. Do the symbols, which reach out to us from thousands of years ago, tell a story? Represent a clan? Mark a trail? Commemorate a success-ful hunting season? The many different beliefs and practices represented here by the petroglyphs make it difficult to interpret the spiritually significant images.

The 2.2-mile lope Rinconada Canyon, an easy-to-hike pathway dotted with sage-brush and wildflowers, will carry you up to the north edge of the canyon then wind you down through the sandy canyon itself. Keep your eyes peeled for the petroglyphs, which are easily found on top of or on the sides of the larger basalt rocks, especially those located on the south-facing slopes. The Volcanoes section of the national monument (5 miles north of I-40, exit 149) features a 3-mile loop path around three cones. The largest volcano here is Vulcan, named after the Roman God of Fire. Visitors can hike the trails at the Volcanoes and Rinconada Canyon, as well as the Piedras Marcadas Canyons, from sunrise to sunset, by simply parking at the gated parking lots just outside the trailheads.

Unser Boulevard NW at Western Trail, Albuquerque, NM; (505) 899-0205; nps.gov/petr/index.htm

SKY CITY CULTURAL CENTER AND HAAK'U MUSEUM ⊙

Sixty miles west of Albuquerque, Sky City, the oldest, continuously operating community in North America, rises from the desert. Built in the 12th century, Acoma Pueblo, as it's also known, sits regally atop a 367-foot sandstone bluff. From its perch 6,460 feet above sea level, the desert landscape and blue skies seem to stretch on forever. This is as close to the clouds as you'll get as you journey along Route 66.

The Acoma have called Sky City home for more than 800 years. Their relatively isolated city, originally only accessible via a treacherous, hand-cut stairway, allowed them to better retain their cherished, customary traditions and afforded them some protection. The Acoma have survived raids by neighboring tribes, Spanish occupation, and epidemics since the pueblo emerged in the 13th century. Today, fewer than 50 tribal members live year-round in the earthen homes of Sky City.

Because Acoma Pueblo is a living, sacred space, Sky City can only be accessed by 90-minute guided, educational tours, which set off from the cultural center. Photography

is restricted. The Acoma people are famous for their pottery, always fired to form very thin walls, and on a tour, you'll meet local artists in action. You'll also visit the 17th-century San Esteban del Rey Mission, one of the few Spanish missions to have survived the Pueblo Revolt of 1680, a successful uprising against the Spanish colonizers (though they returned 12 years later). At the on-site Haak'u Museum, exhibits showcase the history of this isolated pueblo, while also highlighting the most precious of the unique pottery that has been crafted here over the centuries. Locally crafted pottery is for sale throughout the pueblo.

While you're in Sky City, refuel at the Y'aak'a Café, where you'll find a diverse menu of Acoma traditional foods, including delectable fry bread and rich pork and lamb stews and chilies. Y'aak'a means "corn" in Keres, the language of Acoma.

Haaku Road, Acoma Pueblo, NM; (505) 552-7861; acomaskycity.org

EL RANCHO HOTEL 🛏

Few movies define America as a nation as much as Westerns. Celebrating mythic tales of the untamed frontier, they highlighted the good, the bad, and the ugly of the life in the Wild West. At the El Rancho Hotel in Gallup, New Mexico, once the base camp for Western movies in the 1930s and 1940s, you can almost feel the presence of some of the great heroes who fought their battles on the silver screen. Dust off your spurs and saddle up at this historic hotel for a true Wild Western experience, minus the gun slinging.

The beautiful mountain peaks, red rock canyons, and forests surrounding the sleepy desert town made Gallup the perfect backdrop for Westerns. R. E. "Griff" Griffith, brother

of the famous movie director D. W. Griffith, capitalized on both the picture-perfect location, just off Route 66, and the popularity of Westerns, and built the El Rancho Hotel to serve the movie industry in 1936. He harnessed his brother's connections and soon the El Rancho became a home base for the crews and stars filming on location. More than 100 Westerns would be filmed around Gallup, their stars hanging up their 10-gallon hats for the night at El Rancho. John Wayne, Ronald Reagan, Humphrey Bogart, Lucille Ball, Katharine Hepburn, Mae West, W. C. Fields—the hotel echoes with the footsteps of the stars who once called El Rancho home. *Billy the Kid* (1930), *Pursued* (1947), *The Sea of Grass* (1947), *Only the Valiant* (1951), *Escape from Fort Bravo* (1953), and *The Hallelujah Trail* (1965) are just a few of the many Westerns filmed in Gallup. And with so many stars in the sky above the town and within, it's only natural that the on-set gambling, brawling, and drinking continued back at the El Rancho even after the director had called "cut."

New Mexico Department of Tourism

Built of rough-hewn stone, wood, and brick, the rustic El Rancho, with its portico, second-floor balcony, and smoke rising from its chimneys, recalls the classic ranch houses so often portrayed in Western movies. The grand, square lobby appears to have been the benefactor of many a prop department: Navajo rugs lie on the brick floor, deer head trophies are fixed to the columns, a stone fireplace roars. Stamped tin lights hang from the wood-beamed ceiling and two wooden staircases lead up to a second-story balcony, where you'll find autographed photos of El Rancho's most famous guests.

Of course the movie stars and crew members didn't just sleep at El Rancho. They also drank here, at the 49ers Lounge, one of the best bars in the US thanks to its fresh-squeezed margaritas and classic Western decor. Legend has it that Errol Flynn once rode his horse straight up to the bar here, no doubt attracted by the promise of the coldest beers (and the best selection of Mexican brews) in town.

The El Rancho Hotel earns its "Charm of Yesterday" motto. It exudes everything that made the West so wild and wonderful and remains one of the most charming places to spend the night along the Mother Road.

1000 E. Route 66, Gallup, NM; (505) 863-9311; route66hotels.org

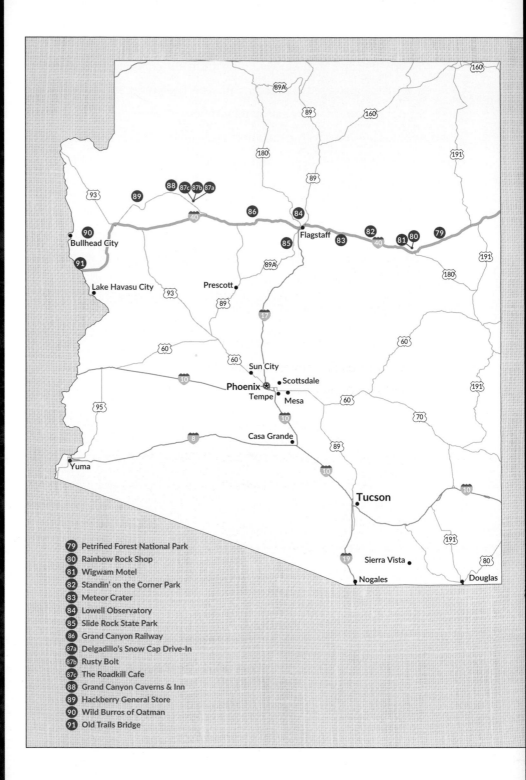

ARIZONA

- 79 Petrified Forest National Park
- 80 Rainbow Rock Shop
- 81 Wigwam Motel
- 82 Standin' on the Corner Park
- 83 Meteor Crater
- 84 Lowell Observatory
- 85 Slide Rock State Park
- 86 Grand Canyon Railway
- 87a Delgadillo's Snow Cap Drive-In
- 87b Rusty Bolt
- 87c The Roadkill Cafe
- 88 Grand Canyon Caverns & Inn
- 89 Hackberry General Store
- 90 Wild Burros of Oatman
- 91 Old Trails Bridge

PETRIFIED FOREST NATIONAL PARK 📷 👟

If you could travel back in a time machine to 225 million years ago, you'd find giant phytosaurs and armadillo-like *Desmatosuchus* wandering through the lush, fern-filled forests of northeastern Arizona. Erupting volcanos in the geologically active zone toppled down trees, covering them in a tomb of ash and debris.

Millions and millions of years then passed, and the buried trees slowly transformed into colorful stones. Wind and water washed away the sands of time, revealing the incredible colorful logs of Petrified Forest National Park.

As the only park in the national park system containing a section of Historic Route 66, it's fitting that the Petrified Forest is so easily drivable, with eight viewing points

National Park Service/Andrew V. Kearns

where you can park your car and soak in the incredible vistas. Driving the 28-mile route that runs through the heart of the 230-square-mile park takes about an hour.

Start at the north end, where several outlooks with unparalleled vistas of the Painted Desert, an awe-inspiring landscape of brilliant badlands named by an expedition under the command of Francisco Vázquez de Coronado that arrived here in 1540, hoping to discover one of the mythical "Seven Cities of Gold." For spectacular views, park at the Tawa Point or Kachina Point trailheads and hike along the rim on the easy, 1-mile Painted Desert Rim Trail. Looking northwest from the trail, it's easy to spot Pilot Rock, the highest point in the park at 6,235 feet high.

At the southern end of the park, the .04-mile Giant Logs Trail loops around some of the biggest and most colorful petrified logs in the park, including the 10-foot-wide "Old Faithful" log. The .75-mile Crystal Forest trail is named after the beautiful, colorful quartz that formed crystals within the hollow logs millions of years ago.

As the park road circles back toward I-40 heading south (though you can't access the interstate at this point), look west toward the right side of the road where a rusted 1932 Studebaker (Stop Number 4) marks the site of the old Route 66 roadbed.

It's tempting to take one of the precious petrified treasures home as a souvenir of your visit, but not only is it illegal to remove petrified wood, legends speak of a dastardly curse that bestows bad luck on anyone who pockets even the smallest of fragments.

1 Park Rd., Petrified Forest, AZ; (928) 524-6228; nps.gov/pefo

RAINBOW ROCK SHOP 🖩

Dare to steal a rock from the Petrified National Forest and you'll face a fine—a minimum of $325 for removal or damage—as well as a curse. For years the Petrified Forest National Park has received returned pieces of pilfered petrified wood tied to tales of misfortune and regret.

Larry Lindahl/Arizona Tourism

If you'd like a souvenir slice of petrified wood, magnificent meteorite, a gem of a geode, or other colorful rocks, head to the Rainbow Rock Shop, where all the beautiful geologic goods on sale were collected legally, from private land surrounding the national park.

PIT STOP PHOTO OP

The dinosaurs that roam the tiny front yard of the Rainbow Rock Shop are far from ferocious. Crafted from chicken wire and concrete, these statues stand at the ready for your prehistoric and iconic Route 66 photo op.

Rainbow Rock Shop is easy to spot: Just keep your eyes peeled for the big green brontosauruses and their triceratops pal that roam the tiny front yard. Life-size cutouts give you the chance to poke your head in and see what you'd look like as a cave dweller.

Inside the shop, specialty rocks are piled high in every corner, with hand-painted signs explaining their origin or other interesting facts, giving the shopping experience here an educational edge. Prices are reasonable, too, with small geodes starting at just 80 cents.

101 Navajo Blvd., Holbrook, AZ; (928) 524-2384

WIGWAM MOTEL 🛏

If you've ever dreamed of sleeping in a wigwam, here's your chance: Holbrook's Wigwam Motel, part of a once-popular hospitality chain built in the early age of road trips, offers an unforgettable, quasi Native American experience with all the conveniences of the modern era.

It all started with Kentucky-born Frank A. Redford. After visiting a Sioux reservation in South Dakota and a popular ice cream shop shaped like an upside-down ice cream cone, he was inspired to build a themed holiday village, capitalizing on the car travel craze. He patented his one-of-a-kind design in 1936, and soon seven locations popped up across the US. Though many of these roadside Americana motels began to disappear in the 1960s and 1970s with the advent of the interstate system, three of the original seven Wigwam Villages remain in existence and operation today: #2 in Cave City, Kentucky; #6 in Holbrook, Arizona; and #7 in San Bernardino, California.

Located on the Historic Route 66, Wigwam Village Motel #6 is arranged as a square, with 15 concrete-and-steel wigwams lining three sides and the main office on the fourth. Enter via the carport, where a hand-painted sign asks the most important question of the day: *Have you slept in a wigwam lately?*

Carol Highsmith

When Chester C. Lewis passed by Wigwam Village Inn #2 in Cave City, Kentucky, a light bulb went off in his head: He purchased the rights to Redford's original, patented design, and opened Wigwam Village Motel #6 here in Holbrook. In a unique royalty agreement, Lewis installed coin-operated radios throughout his Wigwam Village, with every dime inserted for 30 minutes of play sent to Redford as payment.

These mid-century wigwams are framed with wood, frosted with stucco, and shaped more like tepees. No matter the level of authenticity, they offer a getaway experience like no other.

The rooms still feature the original hickory furniture, and in keeping with the authentic early car travel experience, no telephones or wireless Internet access are available. Check out the small room that contains many of Chester Lewis's wacky memorabilia, including a necklace of human teeth of unknown origin, located near the registration desk in the main office.

811 W. Hopi Dr., Holbrook, AZ; (928) 524-3048; sleepinawigwam.com

STANDIN' ON THE CORNER PARK 📷

It was the Eagles' first single and their very first hit, released on May 1, 1972. "Take It Easy" was written by Jackson Browne and Glenn Frey, and recorded with Frey singing lead vocals. Though it peaked at only number 12 on the July 22, 1972, Billboard Hot 100 Chart, the song is listed today as one of the Rock and Roll Hall of Fame's 500 Songs That Shaped Rock and Roll. A poignant reminder to keep your worries in check—*Take it easy, take it easy; Don't let the sound of your own wheels drive you crazy*—this iconic ode to

Howard Brown/Arizona Tourism

PIT STOP PHOTO OP

A selfie at Standin' on the Corner Park in Winslow is obligatory if you're a fan of classic rock.

embracing a more zen attitude is commemorated here, at the corner of Kinsley Avenue and old Route 66 in Winslow, Arizona.

Legend has it that Jackson Browne's car stalled here in Winslow when a pretty young woman passed by in a pickup. Though he never did actually climb into her flatbed Ford, Browne was so struck by her beauty that he added her to the lyrics:

> Well, I'm a standing on a corner
> In Winslow, Arizona
> And such a fine sight to see,
> It's a girl, my Lord, in a flatbed Ford
> slowin' down to take a look at me.
> Come on, baby, don't say maybe,
> I gotta know if your sweet love is
> Gonna save me.
> We may lose and we may win though
> We will never be here again,
> So open up, I'm climbin' in
> So take it easy.

The city of Winslow honored the classic rock anthem with a life-size bronze statue of a man, acoustic guitar by his side, standing on the corner. A trompe l'œil mural located on the storefront behind the statue reflects a fiery blond-haired woman driving off into the distance in her red flatbed Ford pickup truck.

Though the song seems to imply that the man, despite his pleading, was unable to capture the young woman's heart, look up toward the storefront's second floor, where a windowed mural depicts them as a couple, locked in an embrace. An eagle is perched in the window to the left.

Corner of Kinsley Avenue and Historic Route 66 Winslow, Arizona

METEOR CRATER 📷

Be glad you weren't standing here 50,000 years ago when a 300,000-ton meteorite, traveling at a speed of 26,000 miles per hour, collided with the Earth, rocking the center

City of Kingman

of present-day Arizona with the energy of more than 20 million tons of TNT. The sole reminder of this incredible incident is the 550-foot deep Meteor Crater, one of the best preserved meteorite impact sites on the planet.

While you can't hike around the entire rim of the 2.4-mile-circumference crater, you can walk along the self-guided observation paths that run along it, or step onto one of the three viewing platforms where clear, unobstructed views await. Guided tours are offered daily at 15 minutes past the hour. Some of the platforms reach over the rim's edge, adding to the wow factor, while an indoor viewing area offers a glimpse when the outdoor weather conditions are unfriendly. Hiking into the crater is not allowed.

Surprisingly, the crater is privately owned. In the early 1900s, Daniel Barringer, a mining engineer and businessman, was the first to suggest that the crater was produced by the impact of a meteorite, only to be met by skepticism by most geologists at the time, who widely believed the crater was volcanic in origin. Today the crater is privately owned by the Barringer family.

During the 1960s and 1970s, NASA astronauts trained in the moon-like crater to prepare for the Apollo lunar missions. Look for the painted, 6-foot-tall astronaut cut out of a flat panel of wood with a standard US flag for scale.

Interstate 40, Exit 233, Winslow, AZ; (800) 289-5898; meteorcrater.com

LOWELL OBSERVATORY 👟

City dwellers traveling along Route 66 will no doubt be surprised by the starry skies above. Even on the clearest of nights, artificial light from cities obscures natural darkness, but Arizona, with its wide open spaces, is an astronomer's dream.

Look beyond the stars and say "Hello!" to the universe at the Lowell Observatory, one of the oldest observatories in the US. Founded in 1894 by Percival Lowell, a millionaire who was convinced there were canals built by ancient peoples on the planet Mars, the observatory was the first to zoom in on rings of Uranus, the dwarf planet

Pluto, and the comet Halley. The moon was mapped from here, to prepare for the Apollo missions. The telescopes here still peer deep into space, discovering new facets of our constantly expanding universe.

The landmark observatory operates several telescopes at three locations in the Flagstaff area, but the main center, located on the aptly named Mars Hill, just west of downtown Flagstaff, is home to a historic 24-inch Clark refracting telescope and the Pluto Discovery Telescope, used to discover Pluto in 1930.

At the Lowell Observatory, you become the astronomer thanks to vibrant programs, workshops, and guided tours. Gaze at Pluto from the telescope that discovered it; stare into the sun through a specially equipped solar telescope. Navigate the night sky and learn the mythology behind the constellations. See the planets, moon, star clusters, and other deep-space objects from the lens of an early telescope.

Begin your visit in the 6,500-square-foot Steele Visitor Center, where you can catch a tour of one of the many multimedia shows that focus on different aspects of astronomy. Be sure to save some time to see the on-site Rotunda Museum, where displays showcase the discovery of Pluto, the observatory's important role in mapping the moon, and the amazing life and zany theories of founder Percival Lowell.

Flagstaff, where Lowell Observatory is located, became the world's first International Dark-Sky City, on October 24, 2001, for its "exceptional commitment to and success in implementing the ideals of dark sky preservation and/or restoration, and their promotion through quality outdoor lighting" by the International Dark-Sky Association. Lowell researchers continue to glimpse into deep space, unveiling more of the universe's most fascinating mysteries as they search for near-Earth asteroids and extra-solar planets, survey the Kuiper Belt beyond Neptune, and investigate star formations and other puzzling processes in distant galaxies.

1400 W. Mars Hill Rd., Flagstaff, AZ; (928) 774-3358; lowell.edu

SLIDE ROCK STATE PARK

It's a Mother Nature–made water park, complete with red rock beaches, cool, glassy green swimming pools, and crystal-clear waters—minus the chlorine. The highlight: a natural, slick sandstone waterslide that runs down the slippery bed of Oak Creek via chutes and pools galore. There's no better place to escape the desert heat than at Slide Rock State Park, Sedona's splendid swimming hole.

Before it became a state park, this was the Pendley family homestead. Frank Pendley set his stake on these idyllic 43 acres in the early 1900s, eventually pioneering a large apple orchard operation. Though the next generation of the Pendley family sold

Arizona State Parks and Trails

their precious homestead to the state of Arizona in 1987, the park still carries on the apple farming and harvesting traditions of yesteryear.

The world-famous waterslide that the park is named after—Slide Rock—is adjacent to the picture-perfect apple orchard. At 80 feet long and 2.5 to 4 feet wide, with a 7 percent decline from top to bottom, it's a wet, wild, and slippery ride, thanks to abundant algae. A half mile of Oak Creek, one of the few perennial streams in the high desert region of northern Arizona, is open for swimming, wading, and sliding atop the sandstone.

Three hiking trails include the Pendley Homestead Trail, a quarter-mile trail jaunt that rambles through the Pendley family's original apple orchards, homestead house, and apple packing barn, and the Clifftop Nature Trail, an easy trail that will lead you upward to an elevation of 4,966 feet, where you'll find the most spectacular vista of the park. The 0.3-mile Slide Rock Route takes you directly to the Slide Rock swimming hole.

Sliders beware: Depending on the season, Oak Creek's water temps can drop to near freezing, so bring a wetsuit or be prepared to morph into a popsicle. The sandstone rocks below the water's surface are extremely slippery, so bring water shoes or be very careful when crossing on foot.

6871 N. Highway 89A, Sedona, AZ; (928) 282-3034; azstateparks.com/slide-rock

GRAND CANYON RAILWAY

At 277 miles long, a mile deep, and anywhere from 5 to 18 miles across, the Grand Canyon is one of the most awe-inspiring natural wonders of our world. And ever since Route 66 took over its two main streets, the tiny town of Williams, Arizona, has served as a gateway to the immense canyon, offering plenty of motels, restaurants, and gas stations catering to the ever-growing influx of tourists eager to explore a marvel 70 million years in the making.

One of the best ways to discover the Grand Canyon while journeying along Route 66 is to step aboard the Grand Canyon Railway, which departs daily from the historic

Williams Depot. The Grand Canyon Railway made its first 61-mile journey to the South Rim in 1901. It carried countless tourists until 1968, when it lost the battle against car-based tourism to the canyon. But in 1988, it was lovingly restored by a couple from Arizona, Max and Thelma Biegert, and today transports close to 240,000 passengers a year.

Departing daily at 9:30 a.m. from Williams, the train, with its restored, 1920s-era Harriman and mid-century, climate-controlled coaches, travels almost due north to the South Rim of Grand Canyon National Park, arriving at 11:45 a.m. The epic trip measures 65 miles and takes 2 hours and 15 minutes each way, departing the Grand Canyon Depot at 3:30 p.m., returning to the Williams Depot at 5:45 p.m.

As you journey through Canyon Country, you'll witness, from the comfort of your railcar window, changing landscapes that begin with the ponderosa pine forests outside Winslow, followed by the vast prairie, and finally the piñon pine forests as you approach the immense canyon itself. As you travel through the forests, keep your eyes peeled for the elk and mule deer that call this corner of Arizona home. In the high desert, look out for pronghorn, true American natives, since they're found nowhere else in the world; they're also the fastest animal in North America and can sprint up to 70 miles per hour.

Alas, the Wild West is still alive and well along the railway: On the return trip, at the corral near the 100-plus-year-old Grand Canyon Depot, you can count on a crazy cowboy-style shootout as your train departs.

233 N. Grand Canyon Blvd., Williams, AZ; (800) 843-8724; thetrain.com

DELGADILLO'S SNOW CAP DRIVE-IN, THE RUSTY BOLT, AND THE ROADKILL CAFÉ

Seligman is a Route 66 roadside town par excellence. Thought its population barely exceeds 450 people, the fine citizens of this high desert hotspot welcome visitors to their colorful, kitschy main drag.

A former stage stop along the historic Beale's Wagon Road that once shuttled pioneers towards California, it was Route 66 that put Seligman on the map. The 1926 alignment begins at the corner of Lamport Street and East Railroad Avenue and extends along East Railroad Avenue to Main Street then north on Main Street to the corner of Main and Chino Streets.

Seligman was the first town after a long, uninterrupted stretch of the westbound highway. Small mom-and-pop businesses embraced motorists, enticing them with glowing neon signs and colorful storefronts and inviting them to stay for a while. When I-40 took over Route 66's traffic in 1978, so many towns like Seligman turned into ghostly shells of their former selves—some morphed into ghost towns altogether. But Seligman stayed strong thanks to its old-timey charm and friendly hospitality, and it remains a popular stopping point that offers a taste of the Mother

Foodie Find

SNOW CONE FROM DELGADILLO'S

Cool off with a classic snow cone at one of Route 66's most beloved roadside eateries.

Road's heyday. It's no surprise that Pixar modeled the fictional town of Radiator Springs in *Cars* after quirky Seligman.

Three local businesses encapsulate the spirit of Seligman: Delgadillo's Snow Cap, The Rusty Bolt, and the Road Kill Café.

It's impossible to pass by Delgadillo's Snow Cap Drive-In without being enticed by the neon glow of the ice cream cones and the colorful images of banana splits, cherry-topped fudge sundaes, and overflowing root beers that decorate the façade. Built in 1953 out of scrap lumber from the nearby Santa Fe Railroad yard, owner Juan Delgadillo pulled out all the stops to attract passing motorists. He even went so far as to adorn his 1936 Chevrolet hardtop with eyeballs on the front window, horns and plastic flowers galore, and a Christmas tree in the trunk for good measure and park it in front as an unofficial greeter. Over the years, Delgadillo's added more vintage Chevys, googly eyes painted on the windshields, to his car museum within a parking lot. The playful menu here offers "cheeseburgers with cheese," "dead chicken," "oink burger" (burger with bacon), "girl cheese" (grilled cheese), and coffee, with a choice of "today's or yesterday's."

301 W. Route 66, Seligman, AZ; (928) 422-3291

The Rusty Bolt has a similar roadside advertising philosophy: the more over-the-top, the better. This souvenir shop/saloon features a façade literally crawling with mannequins. Some are dressed up as cowboys, others as Wild West–era ladies of the night. Still others look like they were grabbed from the local department store circa 1980 and

planted here in the dead of the night. Marilyn Monroe guards the entrance. Elvis sits on the rear bumper of a candy-pink 1959 Edsel. Choppers line the street front of this popular biker bar.

22345 W. Route 66, Seligman, AZ; (928) 422-0106

No doubt you've already encountered some roadkill along the route. The rustic Roadkill Café, resplendent with the best in taxidermied decor, celebrates those animal lives lost to the highway. Despite the motto here—"You kill it, we grill it!"—and the names of the dishes featured on the menu, none of the meat served here was collected off the side of the road. "Tried-to-Pass-Me-By on Rye" (a.k.a. patty melt), "Long Gone Fawn" (6-ounce sirloin steak), and "The Chicken That Almost Crossed the Road" (fried chicken) are just some of the tasty vittles on the pun-tastic menu.

22830 W. Route 66, Seligman, AZ; (928) 422-3554

CAVE SUITE AND CAVERN GROTTO RESTAURANT AT THE GRAND CANYON CAVERNS AND INN 🍽

It's a claim that zero other motels can make. The Grand Canyon Caverns and Inn contends that its Cave Suite is the "largest, oldest, deepest, darkest, quietest motel room in the world"—and it's not your typical tall tale. Located on a beautiful plateau, smack dab in the middle of more than 3,000,000 acres of the most unspoiled land left on Planet Earth, at an elevation of 5,500 feet and boasting one of the largest dry caverns in the United States approximately 300 feet below the surface, this Route 66 motel/diner/ gift shop/RV campsite/rodeo ring is your one-stop-shop for an incredible overnight adventure. Since it's located close to the Supai Falls and just a short distance to the

Grand Canyon and Colorado River rafting, it's also the ideal base camp for exploring northern Arizona.

While you can always choose to stay in one of the many above-ground rooms for the night, it's the highly sought after Cave Suite here that offers a once-in-a-lifetime escape to the depths of the Grand Canyon. You'll need to take the special elevator 220 feet below ground to reach your cavern abode, where you're guaranteed a restful night thanks to the absolute darkness and quiet.

It took a whopping 65 million years to form this stunning suite. Inside, you'll find all the amenities you need for your night underground, including two double beds, a living room with a queen fold out sofa, a library of old books and magazines such as a *National*

Geographic collection dating back to 1917 and even a record player with records. The suite sleeps up to six people.

No need to worry about suffocating in the suite—air seeps in through the limestone crevices while the rock removes any moisture or impurities—nor do you have to conquer bats, or any other life for that matter, as the only life that's been able to reach these depths needs to descend in the elevator. The temperature stays 72 degrees Fahrenheit year-round.

If you can't fathom sleeping so deep underground, the inn's diner, the Cavern Grotto, gives you the chance to make like a cave person as you munch on an all-you-can-eat buffet 200 feet below the Earth's surface. The American fare here is prepared in the above-ground kitchen and delivered via both elevator and bucket pulley system. With just four tables and a maximum seating capacity capped at sixteen people, this all-you-can-eat adventure is very exclusive, so be sure to make a reservation well in advance.

115 Mile Marker AZ-66, Peach Springs, AZ; (928) 422-3223; gccaverns.com

HACKBERRY GENERAL STORE

Blink and you might miss it. Hackberry, an unincorporated community in Mohave County, Arizona, is just about as close as a town can come before being officially declared a ghost town. Just 68 residential mailboxes are served by the post office in this former mining town, named for a nettle tree found in a spring near the silver mine that sprang up back in 1875.

Centered around the mine, Hackberry was populated by prospectors. But by the early 1900s, the mine closed down, the miners moved on, and the tumbleweeds moved in.

It wasn't until Route 66 rolled down its main drag in 1926 that life returned to the tiny town. Stations were built to service incoming cars and roadside businesses boomed. The small Hackberry General Store opened at a time when it took a full day to get to the nearest town by Model T. Sadly, when Interstate 40 was built, it left Hackberry stranded

16 miles away, without access to so much as an off-ramp. By 1978, the last gas station had closed, most of the fine citizens had moved away, and the ghosts moved in.

Enter itinerant artist and Route 66 icon Bob Waldmire, who set up shop in the dying town, reopening the Hackberry General Store as an unofficial tourist welcoming center and souvenir shop, greeting visitors from near and far.

It's no surprise that this store boasts the "mother lode of mother road memorabilia." The rustic storefront is packed with vintage Mother Road signs and artifacts. Pegasus gas pumps stand at the ready to refill empty tanks. Rusty Model As, a Model T flatbed truck, and a '57 Corvette recall the byway's earliest days to its mid-century heyday. Vintage advertising signs dominate the backyard. Grab one of the refreshing Route 66 root beers and take a minute to pause at the picnic tables by the fish pond.

Inside, visitors naturally trade tales from the road while perusing the many maps, books, signs, and artifacts.

11255 AZ-66, Kingman, AZ; (928) 769-2605; hackberrygeneralstore.com

WILD BURROS OF OATMAN

You'd have to be a real jackass to live in Oatman, Arizona.

Wikimedia Commons

That's because the main drag of this high desert town is overrun by a herd of wild burros.

Once upon a time, Oatman stood among the largest gold producers in the American West. The town teemed with prospectors eager to strike it rich. A whopping 3 million dollars' worth of gold was mined here between 1904 and 1907. Yet another vein of gold was struck in 1910, and the population of tiny Oatman exploded into the thousands.

But then the mines closed and the prospectors fled to the next boomtown, leaving their burros behind. No longer having to work for a living, the donkeys began foraging for food and relearning the ways of their wild ancestors.

By the time Route 66 was replaced with the interstate, more jackasses wandered the streets than locals. Today only about 100 people live in Oatman year-round, and the beloved burros, descendants of the original herd that worked the mines, browse the shops, bray with tourists, and dine au plein air. As one resident explained, "They become like family. We all know their names, and even when they wander in the store, it's hard to get upset with them."

The jackasses here enjoy being hand-fed hay cubes, a.k.a. "burro chow," available for sale at most of the town's saloons and souvenir shops. Bear in mind, however, that these burros are indeed wild, and though they tend to be friendly, they can bite if they're feeling fearful.

Oatman, AZ

OLD TRAILS BRIDGE 📷

Countless families were forced to flee the state of Oklahoma during the devastating Dust Bowl and Depression. Nicknamed "Okies" because so many had narrowly escaped the desperate, dust-strewn, drought-stricken farms of Oklahoma, they traveled westward, along Route 66, toward the so-called promised land of California, hoping to find work and a fresh start. They hoped to find jobs in California, largely in the booming

CALIFORNIA and ARIZONA BORDERS at TOPOCK on the COLORADO RIVER

Wikimedia Commons

agricultural sector, but upon arrival, they faced discrimination as well as miserable working conditions and low wages, if they had been able to find a job at all in the struggling, Great Depression economy.

John Steinbeck's 1939 Pulitzer Prize–winning novel *The Grapes of Wrath* tells the tale of the Joads, a family of sharecroppers who lose both their land and home. They faced no other choice but to pack their life's belongings onto their 1926 Hudson "Super Six" sedan and head west. In Chapter 12, Steinbeck coined the phrase "Mother Road" when he wrote, "Highway 66 is the main migrant road. . . . 66 is the path of a people in flight. . . . 66 is the mother road, the road of flight."

The 1940 film adaptation, directed by John Ford, captures the exact moment that the Joads cross the Colorado River into the so-called promised land of California aboard the old Topock Bridge, also known as the Old Trails Bridge. From 1916 until 1948, this bridge was responsible for shuttling thousands of poverty-stricken families like the Joads across the state line into California.

With its span of 600 feet, the 800-foot-long steel-arched bridge was built in 1914 as part of the National Old Trails Road, Route 66's predecessor. Engineers used a unique cantilever method of construction to create what was the longest, lightest arched bridge in America at its inauguration. By 1926, Route 66 was aligned atop the bridge.

The Old Trails Bridge shuttled cars across the river rapids until the late 1940s when its deck was removed to accommodate a natural gas pipeline and Mother Road traffic was taken over by the interstate highway system.

Listed in the National Register of Historic Places in 1988, this graceful bridge still serves as a poignant reminder of the many people who followed their hopes and dreams westward along the Mother Road.

15130 Historic Route 66, Topock, AZ

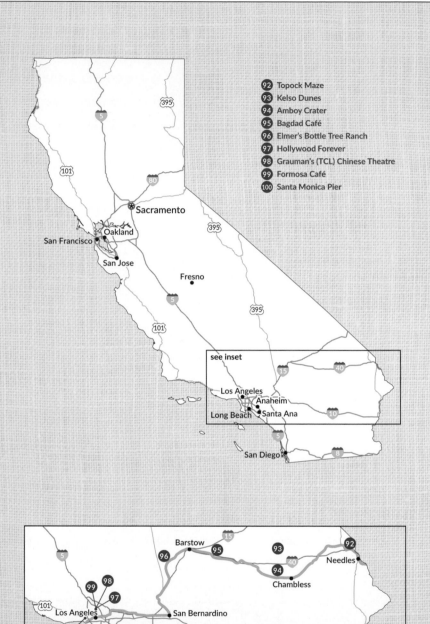

CALIFORNIA

92 Topock Maze
93 Kelso Dunes
94 Amboy Crater
95 Bagdad Café
96 Elmer's Bottle Tree Ranch
97 Hollywood Forever
98 Grauman's (TCL) Chinese Theatre
99 Formosa Café
100 Santa Monica Pier

395

5

101

80

Sacramento

Oakland
San Francisco

San Jose

Fresno

5

101

395

395

see inset

15

40

Los Angeles
Anaheim
Santa Ana
Long Beach

10

San Diego

8

Barstow

15

96

95

93

92

5

94

40

Needles

Chambless

99

98

97

San Bernardino

101

Los Angeles

100

Anaheim

Santa Ana

Long Beach

5

15

10

TOPOCK MAZE 📷

If you're searching for the door to eternity, look no further.

Topock Maze is allegedly a prehistoric portal to the afterlife.

Though no one knows exactly when or why it was created, the modern descendants of the original builders, the Fort Mohave Indians, believe that if you walk along this ancient pathway, you'll slowly enter a peaceful forever. Bad souls tend to get lost among the circling patterns.

Spread over 15 acres, the maze appears to have been just one of many geoglyphs, large designs or motifs created on the ground out of natural elements; in this case, gravel was gathered in mounds to form long, parallel, undulating lines. The removed gravel outlines and emphasizes the lines, which are best viewed from the clouds above. Most of the maze was swept away by the sands of time . . . and the construction of the railroad and Route 66.

14936 THE MYSTIC MAZE OF THE MOJAVE INDIANS NEAR NEEDLES, CALIF.   COPR. FRED HARVEY.

Wikimedia Commons

A placard near the site reads, "Here, upon this land where you now stand, is the Topock Maze; indeed, a cultural site of much importance to the tribe. To this site the AhaMakav warriors returning home from battle first paused for purification before continuing home."

The maze is now fenced off from the public for protection, but you can still gaze upon this mysterious geoglyph by exiting Interstate 40 at Park Moabi Road; head south until it ends then turn and follow the dirt road to the entrance of the mystic maze.

I-40, exit Park Moabi Rd., Needles, CA

KELSO DUNES 👟

In a southern, sand-swept corner of the vast Devils Playground in the Mojave National Preserve, the sand rises, sparkles . . , and sings. The Kelso Dunes are the largest (spread over 45 acres) and highest (reaching up to 600 feet) in the region. Quartz and feldspar were swept into this magnificent formation thousands of years ago, rising into brilliant pink-hued mounds. Bring a magnet and you can gather the superfine grains of black magnetite that accumulate on the crests.

It's the musical phenomenon known as "singing sand" that adds an otherworldly element to a hike on the Kelso Dunes. Climb to the top and slide down the slope and the dunes will boom as your fancy feet set off tiny avalanches that emit low-frequency rumbles.

While the park's Visitor Center is located in the historic Kelso Depot, a lovely mid-1920s-era Mission and Spanish Colonial Revival–style railroad station, the trailhead is at the end of a 3-mile dirt road, accessible from Interstate 40, that splits from Kelbaker Road. It takes about two hours to hike to the top of the closest dune and slide down in song. The 3-mile Kelso Dune Trail takes longer than expected as it's tough to trudge through the sand, but the musical slide down is a breeze. Try to

Mark A. Wilson

plan for a sunrise or sunset hike, when the temps are tolerable and the dunes take on a warm, pink glow.

Kelso-Dunes Rd., Mojave National Preserve, CA 92309

AMBOY CRATER 📷

You've almost reached the end of your Route 66 quest. How about setting off on a journey to the center of the Earth for your next adventure?

Here's your chance to climb into a volcano and set sail on—or at least walk atop—a lake of lava.

Thankfully, this volcano is long extinct, so you won't have to worry about falling victim to the next Pompeii-like situation.

Formed during the Pleistocene epoch, this cinder cone last erupted 10,000 years ago and rests eternally inactive. It rises majestically from the basalt lava plains of the eastern Mojave Desert, about 2.5 miles southwest of the tiny Route 66 town of Amboy.

Jshyun/Flickr.com

To hike the 250-foot-tall Amboy Crater is to hike back into prehistory. You might recognize the 1,508-foot-diameter crater as the spine-tingling backdrop for the 1959 sci-fi movie *Journey to the Center of the Earth*.

The Bureau of Land Management recommends hiking the maintained 3-mile Western Cone Trail that rambles through the lava fields, then winds around the cone's western rim, carrying you along a gentle, sloping path directly toward the center of the crater. Once inside, you can cross the caldera and a lake of lava and climb to the top, where a stunning view of the vast desert, which seems to stretch on forever, awaits.

Though you won't have to worry about the volcano exploding during your visit, you do have to take precautions when it comes to the desert temps, which can reach over 100 degrees Fahrenheit from late spring into early fall. Carry extra water and shield yourself from the sun with proper clothing and sunscreen. The Western Cone Trail takes about two hours to hike, and can be easily accessed from the trailhead located at the Amboy Crater day use parking area, where you'll also find shaded and open picnic tables and public restrooms. If you're not up for setting off on a hike, a scenic overlook on the left side of the parking lot offers a good view of the crater.

Try to plan for a visit during the winter or early spring, when you just might catch the desert in glorious bloom: Wildflowers here sometimes sprout as early as February, depending on winter rains, carpeting the Amboy landscape with unexpected color and beauty.

Crater Road and Route 66, Amboy, CA

BAGDAD CAFÉ 📷 🍽️

The sand-swept, desolate desert town of Newberry Springs feels a lot like Baghdad, Iraq, especially on a hot summer day, when the temperatures reach an average of 107 degrees Fahrenheit. Located in what feels like the middle of nowhere in the western

Mojave Desert of Southern California, at the foot of the Newberry Mountains, about 100 miles south of Death Valley National Park, the town only receives about 10 inches of rain each year though underground aquifers make life possible. In the late-1980s a film crew landed here and put the tiny desert oasis on the map when the quirky German movie *Bagdad Café* became a box office and cult cinema hit.

The movie is actually set in Bagdad, California, another former Route 66 roadside town located 50 miles west. But when Bagdad was bypassed by Interstate 40 in 1973, it was abandoned and eventually razed to the ground. The Sidewinder Café in Newberry Springs would have to play the role of the Bagdad Café. Loosely based on the novella *The Ballad of the Sad Café* (1951) by Carson McCullers, the lonely café, run by an overwhelmed single mom, attracts loners and eccentrics, some just passing through. Others are somehow inclined to stay despite the rugged, remote surroundings. When a German woman leaves her husband, she finds a home here among the colorful characters who call the desert oasis home. The movie was such a hit that it was re-created as a television series starring Whoopi Goldberg as the motelier.

The café remains an oddball outpost on Route 66. It changed its name to the Bagdad Café, capitalizing on the movie's success. Inside, the walls and ceiling are lined with Route 66 memorabilia as well as snapshots of the film's cast and crew. It's still a prime spot for meeting interesting, real-life road-traveling characters, and unlike in the movie, you can count on a good cup of coffee.

46548 National Trails Hwy., Newberry Springs, CA; (760) 257-3101

ELMER'S BOTTLE TREE RANCH ⊙

As a little boy in the 1950s, Elmer Long shared a mutual fascination with his father: collecting colored, vintage glass bottles. The collection grew . . . and grew . . . and then Long's father died. In 2000, Elmer took a long metal pipe and transformed it into a trunk and branches and fashioned the foliage out of beer and soda pop bottles that he had gathered with his father over so many years. From one tree to two to three, an entire enchanted forest erupted here along the Mother Road, an oasis in the heart of California's desert.

Today, you can wander among this forest of trees, an unintentional, outsider-art pop-up in desolate Mojave County. The installation is constantly changing with the seasons, so you'll never meet the same forest on your Route 66 journey. Their blue, green, yellow, and brown glass takes on different hues depending on where the sun is in the sky. When the desert breeze rings through the forest, the glass chimes peacefully. Long still builds every single tree by hand and has taken to adding ornaments that range from bones to bells to hummingbird feeders, making each of the 200-plus trees a unique masterpiece.

Bottle Tree Ranch is free of charge, but leave a tip in the small box and Long, who enjoys chatting with visitors to his upcycled ranch, just might give you a small piece of glass as a souvenir.

24266 National Trails Hwy., Oro Grande, CA

HOLLYWOOD FOREVER 📷

No visit to Hollywood is complete without rubbing elbows with a star or two. While it can prove difficult to spot a celeb out on the town, there is one place where you're

guaranteed to wander among some of the best and brightest stars . . . though they're buried 6 feet underground. Hollywood Forever Cemetery is the final resting place hundreds of fallen stars who made their way from stage to screen . . . to their graves, niches, and sarcophagi . . . toward eternity.

Located on Santa Monica Boulevard, a.k.a. Route 66, in Hollywood proper, the stars resting here aren't far from the sets where so many found stardom in the first place. The cemetery was built in 1899, when Hollywood was still a dream. The studios of Paramount Pictures are located at the south end of the boulevard of broken dreams and looking north, through the cemetery's front gates, the Hollywood sign beckons. The cemetery itself has even played a starring role as the creepy backdrop for several episodes of popular television shows, including *Californication*, *Breaking Bad*, and *Beverly Hills 90210*.

You won't find a greater gathering of Hollywood's founders, writers, directors, and of course, performers, anywhere else on earth. Cecil B. DeMille, Jayne Mansfield, Douglas Fairbanks, Mickey Rooney, and Tyrone Power all rest peacefully here. Gangster Bugsy Siegel is interred in the large mausoleum near a Star of David that you might recognize from the scene in *Rocky III*, whereupon Rocky reads that Kaddish here in the "Alcove of Peace." Rudolph Valentino, who sadly died at the young age of 31, was interred here in a temporary crypt, where he eternally awaits the grand gravestone memorial that he was promised. Of particular note are the graves of Judy Garland, who boasts her very own flower-filled pavilion here; her little dog, Toto, from the *Wizard of Oz*, is memorialized with a bronze statue and inscription, "There's No Place Like Home."

Hollywood Forever's interactive grave guide is the best tool to use when exploring the cemetery. Easily accessible on-the-go via smartphone, it offers not only information on burial locations down to the plot number but also photos and film clips. The cemetery regularly hosts community events, including movie screenings and concerts among the burial plots.

Don't be surprised if you come across tens of sunbathing cats: Hollywood Forever is the home of five feral cat colonies. Peacocks also strut their stuff around the headstones and the ponds are the happy home of other feathered friends, including swans and ducks.

6000 Santa Monica Blvd., Hollywood, CA; (323) 469-1181; hollywoodforever.com/interactive-site-map

GRAUMAN'S CHINESE THEATRE AND THE HOLLYWOOD WALK OF FAME 🔟

On May 18, 1927, thousands of people lined up along Hollywood Boulevard hoping to catch a glimpse of the movie stars arriving here for the most spectacular theater opening in motion picture history.

Theater owner Sid Grauman had opened his first theater in the Yukon in the late 1890s and his Egyptian Theater, also located on Hollywood Boulevard, opened to wide acclaim in 1922. His lavish Chinese Theater, which cost a spectacular $2.1 million to build, was his Hollywood dream come true. More stars have strolled the red carpet here than at any other theater in the world, making it a must-see for anyone speeding through Los Angeles down Route 66.

Grauman sought special permission from the US government to import the temple bells, pagodas, and other artifacts that adorn the over-the-top theater directly from China and employed Chinese artisans to handcraft the many ornate details. As the stars made their way through the entrance with its two massive coral-red columns topped by

wrought-iron masks, they were greeted by a 30-foot-high dragon, carved from stone, and two giant, lions, a.k.a. heavenly guard dogs. Grauman had succeeded in transporting patrons to another place and time, similar to the many swashbuckling movies that premiered in the theater, including Cecil B. DeMille's religious epic *The King of Kings*, which was screened with much acclaim on opening night.

The theater's signature Forecourt of the Stars is one of the most poignant stops in Hollywood, located just off the tail end of Route 66 as it breezes through town to its end point. Hollywood's handprints, footprints, and signatures, left in cement by the stars, span cinematic history. Many of the early imprints also feature messages to the much-beloved "Sid," including Mickey Rooney who wrote in 1938, "To Sid without you, I wouldn't be here" and Humphrey Bogart, who made a death wish in jest with his 1946 imprint, "Sid may you never die, till I kill you." The entire forecourt was the result of an *oops* followed by a light bulb marketing moment: Grauman was giving actress Norma Talmadge a tour of the theatre when she accidentally stepped on wet cement, and the rest is history.

Some of the more intriguing prints include Marilyn Monroe's—she left an earring in the cement when she and Jane Russell made their mark at the premiere of *Gentlemen Prefer Blondes* in 1953—and Betty Grable, who pressed one of her legs, insured at the time for $1 million, into cement memory. George Burns left an imprint of his signature cigar; Mel Brooks added a prosthetic sixth finger to his left hand; Whoopi Goldberg accidentally added a print of one of her dreadlocks, too. The two oldest handprints, dated to the theater's opening day, belong to Douglas Fairbanks and Mary Pickford, Grauman's partners in the venture.

Grauman's Chinese Theatre, now known as the TCL Chinese Theatre, remains a vibrant Hollywood hub, hosting over 50 events a year, including special screenings, imprint ceremonies, and film festivals, and it remains the go-to venue for red carpet movie premieres. Take a tour or, even better, catch the latest hit movie, and soak in the glamour and history that envelop every visitor.

6925 Hollywood Blvd., Hollywood, CA; (323) 463-0879; tclchinesetheatres.com

FORMOSA CAFÉ 🍽

If the walls of the Formosa Café could talk . . . oh, the star-studded tales they could tell. Clark Gable, Marilyn Monroe, and Elvis Presley all sipped—or guzzled—cocktails here, when it was known as the go-to lounge for anyone needing a break from filming at the adjacent Warner Studio, sister studio to the main Warner Bros. Studio in Burbank. From its very beginnings as a trolley car to the popular lounge it remains today, it's a survivor of the golden age of cinema and tells the wild story of West Hollywood.

The former 1902–06 Pacific Electric Red Car trolley was repurposed, parked on what was soon to become Route 66, and began serving up dining fare to rising stars in 1920. Frank Sinatra chowed down on chow mein here as he worked on the set of

From Here to Eternity; Marilyn Monroe was a frequent diner while filming *Some Like It Hot*. Mobsters liked to hang here; the Black Dahlia may or may not have dined here on the night she met her gruesome fate. The walls are lined with the photos of the famous faces that made Formosa a premier Hollywood haunt.

You also might have spotted the café's old-school booths and banquettes at the movies: the intimate Formosa Café was used in a scene in *L.A. Confidential* and, more recently, *La La Land*, both Oscar winners. The café is still in the midst of studios today, attracting a steady stream of celebrities, so don't be surprised if you capture a star sipping a martini barside.

7156 California State Route 2, West Hollywood, CA; (323) 850-9050

SANTA MONICA PIER

It's a picture-perfect ending for the journey of a lifetime. After traveling 2,448 legendary miles, from the busy city streets of downtown Chicago, Illinois, across the prairies and deserts of eight states, through three time zones, you've reached the Promised Land. It took the vast Pacific Ocean to bring Route 66 to such an elegant close. You'll have to walk the final 200 feet, however, to reach the end of the road, marked by a sign at the end of Santa Monica Pier.

Foodie Find

FAIRGROUND FAVORITES AT SANTA MONICA PIER

Celebrate the end of the road with freshly fried funnel cakes, lemonade, and triple-scoop ice cream cones, three fairground favorites.

Route 66 enthusiasts have been debating the true terminus for years. Some argue that the real terminus is on 7th Street in downtown Los Angeles, while other opine that it stands at the intersection of Olympic and Lincoln Boulevards in Santa Monica. Everyone agrees, however, that the landmark Santa Monica Pier is the symbolic finish line.

The Santa Monica Municipal Pier, opened to the public in 1909, was always more than simply a solution to sanitation issues and prime fishing destination: The 1,600-foot-long concrete pier has always been the beautiful backdrop for countless concerts, festive dances, and family fun.

Don't miss a whirl on the 1922 Carousel with its 44 hand-carved horses and serenading calliope. A spin on the solar-powered Ferris wheel offers the best view of the endless ocean, an eternal reminder that the journey never truly ends.

Santa Monica, CA; (310) 458-8900; santamonica.com

GEARHEAD'S GUIDE TO ROUTE 66

A journey along Route 66 from Chicago to Santa Monica gives gearheads the chance to soak in car culture at ever quirky mile.

CAR RACING EXPERIENCE AT THE ROUTE 66 RACEWAY

Route 66 Raceway's *Race Your Ride* experience gives gearheads the chance to test their driving skills against the quarter-mile legends. All you need is a car and a valid driver's license to race down the dragstrip in your own street-legal vehicle.

3200 S. Chicago St., Joliet, IL; (855) 794-7223; route66raceway.com

BOB WALDMIRE'S 1972 VW MICROBUS AT THE ROUTE 66 ASSOCIATION HALL OF FAME AND MUSEUM

In addition to countless Route 66 memorabilia, you'll find two iconic Mother Road vehicles on display at the Route 66 Association Hall of Fame and Museum in Pontiac, Illinois: An orange 1972 Volkswagen microbus, itinerant artist Bob Waldmire's home as he traveled from stop to stop, as well as Waldmire's inventive Road Yacht, a former yellow school bus magically transformed into a mansion on wheels.

10 W. Howard St., Pontiac, IL; (815) 844-4566; il66assoc.org/destination/route-66-association-hall-of-fame-museum

NATIONAL MUSEUM OF TRANSPORTATION

The National Museum of Transportation lies on 42 acres dedicated to car culture and the restoration and preservation of our nation's transportation history. At the Earl C. Lindburg Automobile Center, located within the museum, more than 200 rare vintage vehicles await admiration in their old-fashioned car dealership: Earl C. Lindberg was a

St. Louis Cadillac dealer who also developed the car leasing concept in the US. Plan your visit to coincide with one of the many car shows hosted by the museum.

2933 Barrett Station Rd., St. Louis, MO; (314) 965-6212; transportmuseum association.org

ROUTE 66 CAR MUSEUM

Guy Mace, gearhead extraordinaire, happily shares his collection of more than 70 automobiles at this exceptional private museum. Seven Jaguars, two Rolls Royces, a 1963 Morgan owned by Desert Storm's General Norman Schwarzkopf, a Batmobile, and *the* famous truck from the John Ford movie *The Grapes of Wrath* take visitors on a walk through classic car history.

1634 W. College St., Springfield, MO; (417) 861-8004; 66carmuseum.com

VINTAGE IRON MOTORCYCLE MUSEUM

A stop at the Route 66 Vintage Iron Motorcycle Museum is a motorcyclist must-do. More than 40 vintage motorcycles on display include a 1917 Harley Davidson, 1972 Yamaha world-record jump bike, 2004 Honda world-record jump bike, 1949 Indian Scout, 1949 AJS, and a 1957 Ariel Red Hunter, making it the largest vintage motorcycle collection in the country.

128 S. Main St., Miami, OK; (918) 542-6170; route66vintageiron.com

NATIONAL ROD AND CUSTOM CAR HALL AND AFTON STATION

Afton, Oklahoma, boasts two must-stop sites for car lovers. The National Rod and Custom Car Hall honors Darryl Starbird, a.k.a. "King of the Bubbletop," with a grand display of more than 50 of his most fast-forward car creations, including his signature Predicta bubble top and the space-age Reactor Mach II.

The Eagle D-X Afton Station opened in 1934 to service Route 66 motorists; today it's been transformed into the Afton Station Packard Museum, a privately owned

Mobilus In Mobili/Flickr.com

museum that showcases carefully restored Packards, American automobiles produced from 1899 to 1956.

55251 OK-85A, Afton, OK; (918) 257-4234; darrylstarbird.com

CADILLAC RANCH

Pay tribute to Caddies that have passed on to the great Route 66 in the sky at Cadillac Ranch, an American monument that celebrates the life—and death—of the luxury Cadillac. Buried at an angle corresponding to that of the Great Pyramid of Giza, the cars are constantly being painted and repainted, making every visit unique.

Gouldy99-Flickr.com

Cadillac Ranch is on I-40 (formerly Route 66), just west of the Amarillo city line. Take exit 60 and follow the frontage road on the south side of I-40 east for about 1 mile. Park your car along the shoulder. Open sunrise to sunset; admission is always free.

ROUTE 66 AUTO MUSEUM

Step back into the glory days of Route 66 and meet the cars that once ruled the road—Ford Thunderbirds, a 1930s-era Duesenberg, an all-original 1954 Corvette, and more—at this mom-and-pop, motorhead-friendly museum.

2436 Historic Route 66, Santa Rosa, NM; (575) 472-1966

HOLLYWOOD ON 66

America's byway has played a leading role in several movies since it opened for business at the start of the golden age of the silver screen, while countless Hollywood hopefuls have traveled the route to reach the stars in Los Angeles, California. Here are Route 66's top 12 movie-focused sites.

BOB WALDMIRE'S 1972 VW MICROBUS AT THE ROUTE 66 ASSOCIATION HALL OF FAME AND MUSEUM

A 1962 family road trip to California inspired legendary artist and cartographer Bob Waldmire to make Route 66 his lifelong home. He homesteaded in Arizona, reopened the vintage 1934 Hackberry General Store in the ghost town of Hackberry, Arizona, as a Route 66 tourist attraction, and rambled to and fro on Route 66 aboard his orange 1972 Volkswagen microbus, on display here at the Route 66 Association Hall of Fame and Museum. Waldmire and his beloved bus served as the inspiration for the popular hippie character Fillmore from the 2006 Pixar animated motion picture *Cars*.

10 W. Howard St., Pontiac, IL; (815) 844-4566; il66assoc.org/destination/route-66-association-hall-of-fame-museum

KAN-O-TEX SERVICE STATION

Tow Mater, a.k.a. "the world's best backwards driver," star of the 2006 Pixar movie *Cars* and friend of Fillmore, lives further down Route 66 in Galena, Kansas. You'll find him—a 1951 International Harvester L-170 truck—parked at this circa 1934 filling station and automobile repair shop. An interview with the Disney/Pixar crew and the station's owners is featured on the DVD release of *Cars 2*.

119 N. Main St., Galena, KS; (620) 783-1366

CIRCLE CINEMA AND THE WALK OF FAME

Hollywood officially arrived in Tulsa when the Circle Theatre opened its doors in 1928. It remains one of the best cultural venues in Tulsa, thanks to the loyal group of local movie buffs who worked to restore the theater and redevelop it into a community-focused art house cinema. The Circle Cinema Walk of Fame, located on a sidewalk just outside the theater, honors Oklahoma-born film legends with circular, granite stepping stones. James Garner, Tony Randall, Gene Autry, Joan Crawford, and Brad Pitt are just a few of the featured celebrities with ties to the Sooner State. The cinema also served as the setting for the opening scene of the 1983 hit *The Outsiders*.

10 S. Lewis Ave., Tulsa, OK 74104; (918) 585-3504; circlecinema.com

EL RANCHO HOTEL

The El Rancho Hotel served as the home base for the more than 100 Western movies that filmed in Gallup, New Mexico, in the 1930s and 1940s, including *Billy the Kid* (1930), *Pursued* (1947), *The Sea of Grass* (1947), *Only the Valiant* (1951), *Escape from Fort Bravo* (1953), and *The Hallelujah Trail* (1965). Silver screen legends John Wayne, Ronald Reagan, Humphrey Bogart, Lucille Ball, Katharine Hepburn, Mae West, and W. C. Fields all settled in for the night in this classic ranch-style hotel; their autographed photos line the grand lobby's second-floor balcony. The in-hotel bar was a favorite of Errol Flynn, who once strode in on his horse directly from the movie set to secure a cold beer stat.

1000 E. Route 66, Gallup, NM 87301; (505) 863-9311; route66hotels.org

TWIN ARROWS TRADING POST

Two giant 25-foot arrows mark the spot where the Twin Arrows Trading Post once stood. Built in the late 1940s, Route 66 motorists once stopped here to fill up the tank and dine at the Valentine diner. *Forrest Gump* ran past the Twin Arrows in his race across the US.

Exit 219 off I-40 E in Flagstaff, AZ

Stu Rapley/Flickr.com

LUMBERJACK MAN (J. LAWRENCE WALKUP SKYDOME)

He once stood roadside on Route 66 and played a motionless but memorable bystander in cult road classic *Easy Rider*. Sculpted to serve as an attention-grabbing ad, the Lumberjack Man guarded the Lumberjack Café that Billy (Dennis Hopper) and Wyatt (Peter Fonda) passed by as they rode through Flagstaff. When the café closed, the lumberjack was later relocated here, outside the J. Lawrence Walkup Skydome at Northern Arizona University.

1705 S. San Francisco St., Flagstaff, AZ

OLD TRAILS BRIDGE

Countless cars have crossed the iconic Old Trails Bridge. Long a symbol of the so-called "Okies" forced to flee their state of Oklahoma for the promised land of California because of the devastating Dust Bowl, the bridge was captured on the silver screen in the 1940 film adaptation of *The Grapes of Wrath*, directed by John Ford. As the desperate Joad family crosses the Colorado River into California aboard the 800-foot-long steel-arched bridge, they represented just one of thousands of families that traveled westward along Route 66, hoping for a better future.

15130 Historic Route 66, Topock, AZ

AMBOY CRATER

You might recognize the 1,508-foot-diameter Amboy Crater as the dramatic backdrop for the 1959 sci-fi movie *Journey to the Center of the Earth*. Hollywood magic created the movie's volcanic eruption by setting fires at the center of the crater.

Crater Road and Route 66, Amboy, CA

ROY'S MOTEL AND CAFÉ

Roy's Gasoline, located on Amboy's main drag, is a shining example of roadside mid-century Modern Googie architecture. The 1986 neo-noir *The Hitcher*, *Kalifornia*, the 1993 thriller starring Brad Pitt, and the 2015 horror flick *Southbound* were all filmed here in the tiny desert town with this memorable gas station/motel/café/auto repair shop playing the role of backdrop.

87520 National Trails Hwy., Amboy, CA; (760) 733-1066

Stu Rapley/Flickr.com

BAGDAD CAFÉ

A Hollywood film crew put middle-of-nowhere Newberry Springs on the map when it assigned the town's one and only café a major role in the quirky German movie *Bagdad Café* (1987). Though the movie is set in Bagdad, California, another former Route 66 roadside town located 50 miles west, the former Sidewinder Café in Newberry Springs played the role of the lonely Bagdad Café.

Capitalizing on its newfound fame, the café changed its name to the Bagdad Café and plastered snapshots of the film's cast and crew on its walls.

46548 National Trails Hwy., Newberry Springs, CA; (760) 257-3101

HOLLYWOOD, CA

The last segment of Route 66 cuts right through the heart of Hollywood, gifting motorists with a star-studded ending to the journey of a lifetime. Though the alignment has

Allan Bromberg/Flickr.com

veered from the original, you can still travel along much of the original route. As you enter Hollywood, Route 66 turns onto Santa Monica Boulevard, where you'll find the final resting place of many stars, the Hollywood Forever Cemetery, and the celebrity watering hole/former trolley car, the Formosa Café. No visit to Hollywood is complete without a visit to Grauman's Chinese Theatre and the Hollywood Walk of Fame.

For a picture-perfect view of the iconic Hollywood Sign and a look at the true stars in the wide-open sky, visit the Griffith Observatory, an Art Deco jewel atop the southern slope of Mount Hollywood. The observatory was also the setting for many pivotal scenes in James Dean's most memorable movie, *Rebel Without a Cause* (1955); a bust of Dean commemorates the on-site filming.

2800 E. Observatory Rd., Los Angeles, CA; (213) 473-0800; griffithobservatory.org

NATIVE AMERICAN HISTORY ON ROUTE 66

Learn more about the rituals, beliefs, and longstanding traditions of Native Americans as you journey through time and discover the complicated yet incredibly rich history of America's First People on this six-day Route 66 itinerary.

COLLINSVILLE, IL—ST. LOUIS, MO

DAY 1

Your journey through Native American history and culture begins at **Cahokia Mounds State Historic Site**, once the agricultural, cultural, religious, and economic center of the Mississippi River Valley. Built by the native Mississippians, there are 68 preserved mounds here, as well as an incredible sun calendar known as Woodhenge. Take a guided tour (offered April through November), or rent an iPod, available in the Museum Shop, which will guide you along three scenic trails via an interactive app.

The newly restored **Museum of Western Expansion** (11 N. 4th St., St. Louis, MO; 314-655-1614; nps.gov/jeff/index.htm) mixes historical artifacts with interactive audiovisual displays that document the Native American experience during the opening of the West.

The **Saint Louis Art Museum** (1 Fine Arts Dr., St. Louis, MO; 314-721-0072; slam .org) has been gathering the best of Native North American art from the Northwest coast, arctic, plains, and Southwest since the early 20th century. With over 4,500 pieces on display, it stands as one of the most comprehensive and distinguished collections in the United States. Highlights include numerous Mississippian artworks, including a female figure ceramic vessel and a rare ceramic bottle depicting a panther. The museum also showcases the masterpieces of several contemporary Native artists since the 1970s, including prints and photographs by Fritz Scholder, Mark Henderson, and Wendy Red Star.

ST. LOUIS, MO—TULSA, OK

DAY 2 At the beginning of the 1800s, Native Americans lived on their ancestral lands in the Southwest US. By 1830, enforcement of the Treaty of New Echota, an agreement signed under the provisions of the Indian Removal Act of 1830, led to the forced removal of the few who had dared to stay. As they journeyed thousands of miles to "Indian territory" across the Mississippi River, thousands died along what became known as the Trail of Tears. Tucked away off Route 66 (I-44), just west of Rolla, lies the **Larry Baggett's Trail of Tears Memorial**, an outdoor art installation dedicated to this crime against humanity. Outsider folk artist Larry Baggett incorporated elements of Native American culture, astrology, and natural healing into this eclectic tribute to the many Native Americans who perished along the trail that cuts through this land. A wishing well, a sundial, a white buffalo, and rock gardens arranged to reflect the phases of the moon make for a pensive, peaceful park memorial. To reach the monument, heading west on I-44, exit for Jerome at exit 172 and turn immediately north, then right at Highway D toward Jerome; the memorial is a few hundred yards on the left.

Tulsa's **Gilcrease Museum** (1400 N. Gilcrease Museum Rd., Tulsa, OK; 918-596-2700; gilcrease.org) holds one of the world's most comprehensive collections of American Indian and Western art with a focus on Oklahoma's American Indian history. Surrounded by 475 acres of stunning gardens reflecting gardening styles and techniques from four time periods in the American West, the museum also houses a priceless collection of pre-Columbian arrow and spear heads as well as an archival collection containing over 100,000 books, manuscripts, documents, and maps ranging from 1494 to the present, including a letter dictated and signed by navigator Diego Columbus in 1512. The museum is named after Thomas Gilcrease, an oil entrepreneur

and art collector, who began the collection and founded the museum; Gilcrease grew up in the Creek Nation, located within present-day Oklahoma.

Try to plan your visit to Tulsa for October, when the **Cherokee Art Market** (cherokee artmarket.com) gathers Oklahoma's most elite native artists for a competition to the tune of a $75,000 grand prize. Visitors are welcome to observe the tens of artists in action as they create masterworks of Indian jewelry, pottery, textiles, paintings, and sculptures.

DAY 3

Downtown Oklahoma City's **Red Earth Art Center** (6 Santa Fe Plaza, Oklahoma City, OK; 405-427-5228; redearth.org) invites visitors to experience the traditions and collective spirit of American Indians through the more than 1,400 pieces of art—paintings, carvings, weavings, pottery—that evoke the history and cultural diversity of area tribes. Every June, the urban gallery hosts the Red Earth Native American Cultural Festival, a celebration of the area's vibrant Native American culture: Highlights include the parade showcasing the representatives of more than 100 tribes, all dressed in native regalia, and the two-day powwow that fills the Convention Center Arena with both dance competitions and exhibition dances.

Just outside of Oklahoma City, **Fort Reno** was commissioned by the US government in 1874 as a camp built to protect the Darlington Agency from the uprising that eventually led to the Red River War. The post remained in place post-conflict, controlling the Southern Cheyenne and Southern Arapaho reservation. Guided or self-guided tours wind through the fort's remaining 25 buildings as well as the Post Cemetery, final resting place of not only numerous Native Americans but also German and Italian prisoners of war during the fort's years as a World War II POW camp.

The **Kwahadi Museum of the American Indian** (9151 I-40, Amarillo, TX; 806-335-3175; kwahadi.com) melds Native American cultural traditions of the past and present through its beautiful collections and extensive public programs. Of special note are the displays featuring fine bronze castings by sculptor Tom Knapp and the Cunningham Navajo Rug Collection. Dance performances are planned throughout the year, with peak performances held during the annual Indian Summer Ceremonials (last weekend in September through October) and the Winter Night Ceremonials in January; call ahead to reserve tickets.

DAY 4

The Kewa people are well known for their beautiful arts and crafts, all of which reflect their most cherished traditions and the surrounding nature that sustains their way of life. Residents here have somehow managed to hold tight to religious and cultural practices, despite Spanish colonialism, and the routing of the railroad and Route 66. Ever since the Mother Road was routed through **Kewa Pueblo** in 1926, its residents have been offering their fine, handcrafted jewelry for sale at roadside stands. Though the old Pueblo is on the National Register of Historic Places, it remains the vibrant home of more than 3,600 tribal members. Explore the plazas, the Spanish Mission-style church located on the edge of the pueblo and the popular, two-story trading post, erected in 1881: Today it serves as an arts incubator and a place for the tribe's artisans to showcase their fine work. On Labor Day weekend, approximately 400 Native American artists from across the US convene here for the annual **Santo Domingo Arts and Crafts Market.**

New Mexico is home to 19 Pueblo tribes; each Pueblo is a sovereign nation. Albuquerque's **Indian Pueblo Cultural Center** (2401 12th St. NW, Albuquerque, NM; 866-855-7902; indianpueblo.org) *We Are of This Place: The Pueblo Story* permanent exhibit tells the story of the Pueblo people's legacy of resilience through the words and voices of its peoples. Rotating exhibits expand upon the core values—love, respect, compassion, faith, understanding, spirituality, balance, peace, and empathy—as seen through art and culture.

Dine at the museum's in-house **Pueblo Harvest Café**, a full-service restaurant and bakery where New Native American cuisine is brought to the table with traditional, seasonal Pueblo flavors and contemporary cooking methods. Reserve a table on the patio for breathtaking views of the Sandia Mountains. Pueblo Harvest Café is open for breakfast, lunch, happy hour, and dinner Monday through Saturday and for brunch on Sunday.

The **Gathering of Nations Powwow** (gatheringofnations.com), hosted the last weekend in April at the University of New Mexico's WisePies Arena, is the world's largest: The two-day event invites everyone to experience powerful Native American dancing with more than 2,500 indigenous dancers and singers representing more than 500 tribes from Canada and the United States. The gathering's Indian Traders Market displays the fine arts and crafts of more than 800 artists, crafters, and traders.

ALBUQUERQUE, NM—PEACH SPRINGS, AZ

DAY 5

More than 20,000 images carved in stones across the **Petroglyph National Monument** recall the spirits of the ancient peoples who created them. Park staff at the Visitor Center can recommend which trail will best fit your time frame and hiking ability and provide you with maps. The 2.2-mile Rinconada Canyon Trail is perhaps the easiest to hike: Dotted with sagebrush and wildflowers, you'll ascend to the north edge of the canyon then wind through the sandy canyon itself. Petroglyphs are easily found on the larger basalt rocks, especially those located on the south-facing slope.

New Mexico Department of Tourism

Just 60 miles west of Albuquerque, **Sky City**, the oldest continuously operating community in North America, sits regally atop a 367-foot sandstone bluff. Home of the Acoma peoples for more than 800 years, the city was originally only accessible via a treacherous, hand-cut stairway. Today fewer than 50 tribal members live year-round in the earthen homes of this living, sacred space. Ninety-minute guided educational tours set off from the cultural center. The onsite **Haak'u Museum** shares the history of this isolated pueblo, while also highlighting the most precious of the unique pottery that has been crafted here over the centuries. Locally crafted pottery is for sale throughout the pueblo.

While you're in Sky City, refuel at the **Y'aak'a Café**, where you'll find a diverse menu of Acoma traditional foods, including delectable fry bread and rich pork and lamb stews and chilies.

Opened by the Hualapai Tribe in 2007, the **Grand Canyon Skywalk** (888-868-9378; grandcanyonwest.com) is a horseshoe-shape cantilever bridge that gives visitors the chance to look directly down into the depths of Grand Canyon West through the clear glass walk that juts 70 feet past the rim of the Grand Canyon, 4,000 feet above the Colorado River. Also on site is the **Sa' Nyu Wa** restaurant, where guests can dig into unique fusion of Southwest and Asian cuisine combined with traditional Hualapai tribal dishes served with the canyon as a backdrop thanks to the floor-to-ceiling windows overlooking the West Rim.

PEACH SPRINGS, AZ—LOS ANGELES, CA

DAY 6

The Fort Mohave Indians, builders of the intricate **Topock Maze**, believe that if you walk along the intricate, mystical pathway, you'll be guided toward eternity. The maze is a geoglyph, a large design created on the ground, out of natural elements. Legend states that AhaMakav warriors, returning from battle, paused here for purification before continuing home.

Before reaching the end of Route 66 in Santa Monica, pop into the **Autry Museum of the American Southwest** (4700 Western Heritage Way, Los Angeles, CA; 323-667-2000; theautry.org), established in 1988 by singing cowboy Gene Autry. The museum's 238,000-piece *Southwest Museum of the American Indian Collection* represents work by indigenous peoples from Alaska to South America, though the focus is on the cultures of California and the Southwestern US. Catch a show by Native Voices at the Autry (theautry.org/events/signature-programs/native-voices), the only Equity theater company devoted exclusively to developing and producing new works for the stage by Native American, Alaska Natives, and First Nations playwrights.

MOTHER ROAD FOR MUSIC LOVERS

Countless musical legends, in genres as diverse as blues, jazz, folk, and rock, have found inspiration along Route 66. Experience the echoes of your favorite singers and song-writers at these top 10 sites for music lovers on the Mother Road.

ELVIS ROOM AT THE BEST WESTERN ROUTE 66 RAIL HAVEN

In 1956, Elvis Presley crashed here in Room 409, just after he hit the stage of the nearby Shine Mosque. No other motel along Route 66 gives guests the chance to count sheep from the comfort of a '57 Chevy convertible bed.

203 S. Glenstone Ave., Springfield, MO; (417) 866-1963; bestwestern.com

WOODY GUTHRIE CENTER

Woody Guthrie's social-justice-themed music inspired countless travelers along the Mother Road. Located in the former home of the Tulsa Paper Company, the Woody Guthrie Center houses the world's largest collection of material relating to Guthrie's life and hosts live music perfor-mances with a focus on country, roots-rock, folk, bluegrass, and blues.

102 E. Mathew B. Brady St., Tulsa, OK; (918) 574-2710; woodyguthriecenter.org

Allison Meier/Flickr.com

CAIN'S BALLROOM

Considered one of the top live music performance venues in the world today, Cain's Ballroom's springy maple-wood dance floor vibrates along with all the foot stomping and toe tapping. The programming remains delightfully eclectic, so you never who your ears will encounter in this legendary music hall.

423 N. Main St., Tulsa, OK; (918) 584-2306; cainsballroom.com

ARCADIA ROUND BARN

Built to house animals and hay, the Arcadia Round Barn was so beautiful upon completion that three of the young men who helped raise it declared it a dance hall. Music still reverberates through the rounded rafters every second Sunday of the month, when the accidentally acoustic barn hosts a popular concert series.

07 OK-66, Arcadia, OK; (405) 396-0824; arcadiaroundbarn.com

MUSICAL ROAD OF TIJERAS

Give your car a chance to carry a tune on this magically musical stretch of highway: Follow the speed limit and your car will sing the song "America the Beautiful," using its wheels as a uniquely Route 66 instrument.

The Musical Road of Tijeras is labeled as eastbound Route 333 (formerly Route 66) and is located between mile markers 4 and 5, near exit 170, in Tijeras, New Mexico.

KIMO THEATER

Built as a movie and vaudeville theater in 1927, the KiMo Theater, long considered a symbol of Albuquerque, today offers a rich variety of cultural programming and musical entertainment of all genres.

423 Central Ave. NW, Albuquerque, NM; (505) 768-3522; kimotickets.com

Kent Kanouse/Flickr.com

STANDIN' ON THE CORNER PARK

Live the Eagles' very first single, "Take It Easy," by standing on *the* corner in Winslow, Arizona.

Corner of Kinsley Avenue and Historic Route 66, Winslow, AZ

KELSO DUNES

Thanks to the musical phenomenon known as "singing sand," the Kelso Dunes will boom as your fancy feet slide down, setting off tiny avalanches that emit a low-frequency, rumbling tune like no other.

Kelso-Dunes Rd., Mojave National Preserve, CA

THE TROUBADOUR

Though it opened its doors as a coffeehouse back in 1957, it soon became a hot hub for emerging musical artists. From hardcore rock to country to folk music, singer-songwriters of all genres still showcase their up-and-coming songs at the one and only Troubadour.

9081 N. Santa Monica Blvd., West Hollywood, CA; troubadour.com

MCCABES GUITAR SHOP

McCabes holds the largest selection of stringed things to make music with in the state of California. The shop also hosts concerts in its intimate back room, one of the most exclusive and treasured listening spaces in the US.

3101 Pico Blvd., Santa Monica, CA; www1.mccabes.com

THE MOTHER ROAD WITH KIDS

While kids will find something to love at every stop along the Mother Road, here are the top stops for road trippin' families.

GEMINI GIANT

The Gemini Giant stands forever ready for takeoff, rocket in hand, like an oversize toy action figure. The giant's Launching Pad, a circa 1965 diner where he fuels up on pre-launch burgers, fries, and ice cream cones, is located just next door.

810 E. Baltimore St., Wilmington, IL

SKY VIEW DRIVE-IN

Kids can trade their tablets for a screen under the stars at this old-school drive-in. Stock up on movie treats at the snack bar and stay parked for a (free!) second screening.

1500 Old Route 66, N. Litchfield, IL; (217) 324-4451; litchfieldskyview.com

HENRY'S RABBIT RANCH

Your kids are bound to fall in love with all the adorable bunny rabbits that call this quirky, sprawling ranch home.

1107 Historic Old Route 66, Staunton, IL; (618) 635-5655; henrysroute66.com

BROOKS CATSUP BOTTLE

You just can't miss "The World's Largest Catsup Bottle." Standing at 70 feet tall, this former water tower will leave everyone in your car craving catsup and fries.

800 S. Morrison Ave., Collinsville, IL; catsupbottle.com

GATEWAY ARCH

Take the four-minute tram ride up the leg of the arch to the observation deck where, on a clear day, you can see up to 30 miles in every direction.

St. Louis, MO; (877) 982-1410; gatewayarch.com

MERAMEC CAVERNS

Kids will truly feel as if they are on a journey to the center of the Earth as they tour the seven levels of this incredible 400-million-year-old cave system.

1135 Highway W., Sullivan, MO; (573) 468-2283; americascave.com

KAN-O-TEX SERVICE STATION—HOME OF TOW MATER

Tow Mater, "the world's best backwards driver," star of the 2006 Pixar movie *Cars*, is permanently parked at this Historic Route 66 service station in Galena, Kansas.

119 N. Main St., Galena, KS; (620) 783-1366

ED GALLOWAY'S TOTEM POLE PARK

Wander among the totem poles adorned with birds, trees, arrowheads, and other Native American motifs at this the largest open-air folk art museum in the state of Oklahoma.

21310 E. Hwy. 28A, Chelsea, OK; (918) 283-8035; rchs1.org/totem-pole-park

BLUE WHALE OF CATOOSA

Step into the mouth of the 80-foot-long sperm whale stranded far from the ocean here in tiny Catoosa. The big, brilliant Blue Whale of Catoosa is a must-meet icon of the Mother Road.

2600 Route 66, Catoosa, OK; bluewhaleroute66.com

POPS SODA RANCH

There's a flavor—more than 700 in stock!—to fit every taste at this unofficial soda pop mecca of America.

660 OK-66, Arcadia, OK; (405) 928-7677; POPS66.com

FIRST PUBLIC SCHOOLHOUSE

Take a guided tour of the earliest one-room schoolhouse in the Oklahoma Territory. Children of all ages were grouped together in this one room, learning the basics of reading, writing, and arithmetic under the command of a single local school teacher. Be on your best behavior or you just might have to don the dunce cap!

24 E. 2nd St., Edmond, OK; (405) 715-1889; edmondhistory.org/1889-territorial-schoolhouse

GLENRIO GHOST TOWN

Be on the lookout for wandering spirits as you stroll the windswept, empty streets of eerie, long-abandoned Glenrio.

Glenrio, TX

BLUE HOLE

Jump into the Blue Hole of Santa Rosa, a giant, hourglass-shape, 80-foot-diameter swimming hole that miraculously formed thousands of years ago here, in the middle of the high desert.

Route 66, Santa Rosa, NM; (575) 472-3763; santarosabluehole.com

ZOZOBRA

Every late summer in Santa Fe, Zozobra, a 50-foot-tall marionette, tries to rob local children of their happiness. He takes up residence every September in Fort Marcy Park only to be burned at the stake. The Burning of Zozobra is one of Santa Fe's largest and happiest events, taking place annually on the Friday before Labor Day; if you can't make the annual celebration, write down your worry on a slip of paper and leave it in the "gloom box" found in the offices of the *Santa Fe Reporter* (132 E. Marcy St.) in the weeks leading up to the burn.

Santa Fe, NM

MUSICAL ROAD OF TIJERAS

Sing along as you drive this quarter-mile stretch in tiny Tijeras, New Mexico: Follow the speed limit of 45 miles per hour and your car's wheels will vibrate to the tune of "America the Beautiful."

The Musical Road of Tijeras is labeled as eastbound Route 333 (formerly Route 66) and is located between mile markers 4 and 5, near exit 170 in Tijeras, NM.

AMERICAN INTERNATIONAL RATTLESNAKE MUSEUM

Spend some up close and personal time with incredible yet often misunderstood rattlesnakes and unveil the myths surrounding the serpents.

202 San Felipe St. NW, Albuquerque, NM; (505) 242-6569; rattlesnakes.com

PETRIFIED FOREST NATIONAL PARK

Hike the easy, 1-mile Painted Desert Rim Trail through the awe-inspiring landscape of brilliant badlands.

1 Park Rd., Petrified Forest, AZ; (928) 524-6228; nps.gov/pefo

RAINBOW ROCK SHOP

Pay a visit to the Rainbow Rock Shop, where you'll find all the colorful rocks you need to start your very own rock collection.

101 Navajo Blvd., Holbrook, AZ; (928) 524-2384

WIGWAM MOTEL

Why settle for a boring old chain motel room when you can spend the night inside your very own wigwam?

811 W. Hopi Dr., Holbrook, AZ; (928) 524-3048; sleepinawigwam.com

SLIDE ROCK STATE PARK

While away a hot afternoon in the crystal clear, cool waters of Sedona's nature-made water park.

6871 N. Highway 89A, Sedona, AZ; (928) 282-3034; azstateparks.com/slide-rock

GRAND CANYON RAILWAY

All aboard the Grand Canyon Railway for a breathtaking journey to the South Rim of Grand Canyon. Watch out for the dastardly cowboys who find themselves in a Wild West–style depot at every return trip departure.

(800) 843-8724; thetrain.com

ROADKILL CAFÉ AND DELGADILLO'S SNOW CAP

Seligman stands as a Route 66 roadside town par excellence. Take your pick from the mock-roadkill menu at the meat-lovers Roadkill Café and cool off with a cone at the ever-popular Delgadillo's Snow Cap.

Roadkill Café, 22830 W. Route 66, Seligman, AZ; (928) 422-3554

Delgadillo's Snow Cap Drive-In, 301 W. Route 66, Seligman, AZ; (928) 422-3291

Karlis Dambrans/Flickr.com

WILD BURROS OF OATMAN

A wild and wacky pack of burros has taken over Oatman's Main Street. Kids can purchase "burro chow" from any local store and hand-feed the always-hungry herd.

Oatman, AZ

ELMER'S BOTTLE TREE RANCH

Explore an enchanted forest of more than 200 trees in the middle of sand-swept Mojave County. This unique folk art installation is bound to inspire your kids to create their own upcycled masterpiece.

24266 National Trails Hwy.; Oro Grande, CA

GRAUMAN'S CHINESE THEATRE AND THE HOLLYWOOD WALK OF FAME

Kids will love seeing if their handprints fit with those of the stars. Challenge them to spot the non-human celebrities that have cemented their prints into eternity: Big Bird, Godzilla, the Muppets, and more animated friends have all left their eternal mark on the historic Hollywood Walk of Fame.

6925 Hollywood Blvd., Hollywood, CA; (323) 463-0879; tclchinesetheatres.com

SANTA MONICA PIER

The last stop on the road is a kiddie paradise on the Pacific. Take a spin on the classic carousel, step into the toothy mouth of a twirling shark, and swirl up into the sky on the fantastic Ferris wheel for a view of the seemingly never-ending ocean beyond Route 66.

Santa Monica, CA; (310) 458-8900; santamonica.com

NATURAL WONDERS OF ROUTE 66

Explore the Southwest's most inspiring natural wonders on this seven-day itinerary. Dive into a shimmering sinkhole, walk along the rim of a volcanic crater, slide down the rocks at a nature-made water park, and more as you meet Route 66's wildest roadside attractions.

PALO DURO CANYON, CANYON, TX

DAY 1

Your journey to Route 66's most amazing natural wonders begins here at **Palo Duro Canyon**, in the heart of the Texas Panhandle. Nature lovers and artists looking for inspiration have long hiked this second-largest canyon in the US, including painter Georgia O'Keeffe, who remarked, "It is a burning, seething cauldron, filled with dramatic light and color." While the best way to experience the canyon is by foot, mountain bike, or horse, thanks to more than 30 miles of hiking, biking, and equestrian trails, you can also explore by car. The Visitor Center offers spectacular views. Spend the night in one of the three cabins on the canyon's rim, or four limited-service cabins on the canyon floor, or be daring and check into one of the primitive drive-up, equestrian, or backpack camping sites. Too hungry to wait for a campfire to cook up your dinner? Take on the steak challenge at the The Big

Wikimedia Commons

Texan Steak Ranch, where a super-size steak is free to anyone who manages to down all 4.5 pounds of steak and the accompanying sides in one hour or less.

CANYON, TX—BLUE HOLE OF SANTA ROSA, NM

DAY 2

If you're looking to cool off after spending so much time under the hot desert sun, jump into a gem: The **Blue Hole of Santa Rosa** is a giant, hourglass-shape, 80-foot-diameter swimming hole formed thousands of years ago here, in the middle of the high desert. Everyone is welcome to swim in its glistening, deep-blue waters and enjoy the cool, constant 64-degree Fahrenheit temperature, but the only way to reach the bottom is via scuba diving: The Blue Hole's

New Mexico Department of Tourism

diameter expands to 130 feet at its maximum depth, almost 80 feet below the desert surface. Located just off old Route 66, the Blue Hole is open 24/7 for swimmers. Divers will need a permit, which is available at an on-site scuba shop along with rental equipment; it's only open sporadically, so call ahead.

After your swim, drive in to the retro classic Comet II Drive-In (1257 Historic Route 66, Santa Rosa, NM; 575-472-3663) for a plate of their signature smothered burritos.

SANTA ROSA, NM–ALBUQUERQUE, NM

DAY 3

Today's adventure begins with a hike along the 2.2-mile Rinconada Canyon Trail at **Petroglyph National Monument**. The Rinconada Canyon, an easy-to-hike pathway dotted with sagebrush and wildflowers, will carry you up to the north edge of the canyon, then wind you down through the sandy canyon itself. Keep your eyes peeled for the petroglyphs, which are easily found on top of or on the sides of the larger basalt rocks, especially those located on the south-facing slopes. If you're up for more adventure, drive to the volcanoes section of the national monument (5 miles north of I-40, exit 149) and hike the 3-mile loop path that winds around three volcanic cones.

Settle in for the night at the historic **Los Poblanos Historic Inn and Organic Farm**. Originally inhabited by the ancient Anasazi, these idyllic acres were transformed into an experimental farm in the 1930s. Today the regal adobe ranch house serves as the 50-room boutique-style inn, and the farm's focus has shifted to organic, sustainable agriculture. Sign up for one of the many workshops or even volunteer on the farm, planting, weeding, or harvesting organically grown produce for part of your stay.

ALBUQUERQUE, NM—PETRIFIED FOREST NATIONAL PARK

DAY 4

The **Petrified Forest National Park** is easily drivable, with eight viewing points along a 28-mile route. Park at the Tawa Point or Kachina Point trailheads and hike along the rim on the easy, 1-mile Painted Desert Rim Trail. At the southern end of the park, the .04-mile Giant Logs Trail loops around some of biggest and most colorful petrified logs in the park, including the 10-foot-wide "Old Faithful" log. The .75-mile Crystal Forest trail is named after the beautiful, colorful quartz that formed crystals within the hollow logs millions of years ago.

It's tempting to take one of the precious petrified treasures home as a souvenir of your visit, but it's illegal to remove petrified wood. Even worse than paying a stiff fine, legends speak of a dastardly curse that bestows bad luck on anyone who pockets even the smallest of fragments. Instead, stop by the nearby **Rainbow Rock Shop**, where all the beautiful geologic goods on sale were collected legally, from private land surrounding the national park.

Backcountry camping is allowed within the Petrified Forest National Wilderness Area; outside of the park, you'll find plenty of hotels and motels.

HOLBROOK, AZ—PEACH SPRINGS, AZ

DAY 5

From Holbrook, journey through space and time to Winslow, Arizona, and visit Meteor Crater, one of the best-preserved meteorite impact sites on the planet. While you can't hike along the entire rim of the 2.4-mile-circumference crater, you can stop at the self-guided observation paths. Guided tours are offered daily at 15 minutes past the hour.

Cool off at **Slide Rock State Park**, a.k.a. Mother Nature's water park. The natural, slick sandstone waterslide that runs down the slippery bed of Oak Creek make this Sedona's splendid swimming hole. A half mile of Oak Creek, one of the few perennial streams in the high desert region of northern Arizona, is open for swimming and wading. Three hiking trails include the Pendley Homestead Trail, a quarter-mile trail jaunt that rambles through the orchards at the adjacent, apple-growing former homestead house; the Clifftop Nature Trail will lead you upward to an elevation of 4,966 feet, where you'll find the most sweeping vista of the park.

Tuck in for the night in the largest, oldest, deepest, darkest, quietest motel room in the world, the **Cave Suite at Grand Canyon Caverns and Inn**. Though you can always choose to stay in one of the many aboveground rooms for the night, the Cave Suite offers a once-in-a-lifetime escape to the depths of the Grand Canyon via an elevator that reaches 220 feet below ground. Enjoy dinner at the inn's Cavern Grotto restaurant, where an all-you-can eat buffet situated 200 feet below the Earth's surface offers delicious American fare.

DAY 6

All aboard! With daily, 9:30 a.m. departures from Williams, the **Grand Canyon Railway** is one of the easiest ways to explore the breathtaking beauty of Canyon Country. From the comfort of your coach, you'll travel to the South Rim of Grand Canyon National Park, arriving at 11:45 a.m. As you journey through the changing landscapes that begin with the ponderosa pine forests outside Winslow, followed by the vast prairie, and finally the piñon pine forests as you approach the immense canyon itself, be on the lookout for pronghorn.

Make the most of your layover and arrange for a guided motor coach tour of the South Rim's most significant sites. Tours work in conjunction with the train's schedule

Jill McCoomber/Arizona Tourism

and allow for plenty of time to explore the historic Grand Canyon Village. The return trip departs from the Grand Canyon Depot at 3:30 p.m., returning to the Williams Depot at 5:45 p.m.

Before crossing the state line into California, plan for some up close and personal time with the herd of **wild burros** that run wild in Oatman, Arizona. Descendants of the original herd that worked the local mines, these jackasses appear to be regular tourists as they sometimes pop into the souvenir shops on the main drag hoping to be greeted with hay cubes.

KELSO DUNES, CA—AMBOY CRATER, CA

DAY 7

Located in the Mojave National Preserve, the sand rises, sparkles . . . and sings at the **Kelso Dunes**, the largest and highest—reaching up to 600 feet—dunes in the region. Park at the trailhead found at the end of the 3-mile dirt road, accessible from Interstate 40, which splits from Kelbaker Road. The 3-mile trail takes a few hours to hike as it's tough to trudge through the sand, but the musical slide down is a breeze.

"Mike" Michael L. Baird/Flickr.com

If you've ever dreamed of setting off on a journey to the center of the Earth, a hike to the top of the 250-foot-tall **Amboy Crater** features the sci-fi-worthy, 3-mile Western Cone Trail that will transport you through lava fields to the winding western rim of a cinder cone. Once you're inside the crater, cross the caldera and the lava lake and climb to the crater's peak, where a stunning view of the vast desert seems to stretch on for eternity.

SPEEDY 66: CHICAGO TO SANTA MONICA IN SIX DAYS

Tight on time but feeling the need for speed on the wide-open Mother Road? Buckle up and set off on the drive of your life. This time-sensitive itinerary will take you to over 45 of Route 66's most iconic stops in just six days.

CHICAGO, IL—CUBA, MO

DAY 1

Wake up early and head in for breakfast at **Lou Mitchell's**, the unofficial Route 66 starting point in downtown Chicago. Meet up with the **Gemini Giant** in Wilmington, before he launches off into space, then bumble over the **Auburn Brick Road**, one of the last remaining tracts of Route 66 with its original pavement intact. Enjoy Greek-American diner fare for lunch at the longest-operating restaurant along Route 66, the **Ariston Café**. As you approach St. Louis, pause for a moment on the historic **Chain of Rocks Bridge**, where you'll have a nice view of the **Gateway Arch**. Cool off with a concrete at **Ted Drewes Frozen Custard**. Stop for a tour of the glorious **Meramec Caverns**. Snuggle in one of the **Wagon Wheel Motel**'s cozy cottages for the night in Cuba.

CUBA, MO—MIAMI, OK

DAY 2

Rise with the sun and speed out of Cuba early in the morning. Plan for a pit stop in downtown Springfield, Missouri, and make sure to peek inside the beautiful **Gillioz Theatre**. You don't even have to leave your car for a tour of **Wilson's Creek National Battlefield Park** thanks to the 4.9-mile paved tour road with its eight interpretive stops at significant points. A ride through downtown Joplin is a must; be sure to pass by **Bonnie and Clyde's Garage Hideout**. Say hello to

Tow Mater at his vintage **Kan-O-Tex Service Station** in Galena, Kansas, before landing in Miami, Oklahoma. Ramble toward the **Ribbon Road** and try to catch a performance at the **Coleman Theatre**. Dinner calls for the burgers that everyone goes cuckoo over at Waylan's Ku-Ku Burger (915 S. Main St., Miami, OK; 918-542-1696), a mid-century fast food drive-in.

MIAMI, OK—AMARILLO, TX

DAY 3

Rise and shine early so you can make it to **Ed Galloway's Totem Pole Park** in Chelsea for a picnic breakfast beside the World's Largest Concrete Totem Pole. Quick stops at two Route 66 icons—the **Blue Whale of Catoosa** and the **Arcadia Round Barn**—are in order before digging into a Triple Pig Sickle Sandwich at **Jigg's Smoke House** in Clinton. (Grab a few pounds of the house-made beef jerky for the road!) Pay a visit to the **Conoco Tower Station** in Shamrock, perhaps the most elegant vintage gas station along the route. You won't have to leave your car to experience the magnificence of Texas's largest canyon, the **Palo Duro Canyon**: It takes about 45 minutes to drive from the Visitor Center to the rim to the basin and back. Pause for a moment at **Cadillac Ranch**, a folksy monument to motordom, before heading to the **Big Texan** for a steak dinner, and a dip in the Texas-shape swimming pool and overnight at the adjacent Big Texan Motel.

AMARILLO, TX—GALLUP, NM

DAY 4

Breakfast at Route 66's halfway point, the **Midpoint Café** in Adrian, Texas. Stop and stroll the eerie empty streets of the **Glenrio Ghost Town**, then cross the border in New Mexico and cool off at the **Blue Hole** of Santa Rosa. Head into Santa Fe to tour the oldest church in the United States, the **San Miguel Chapel,** then feast on the flavors of the Southwest at the charming La Plazuela de la Fonda, **La Fonda on the Plaza**'s acclaimed, in-hotel restaurant. At **Petroglyph National Monument**, you can hike the easy 2.2-mile Rinconada Canyon loop that features petroglyphs galore; alternatively, head to the volcanoes section and set off on the 3-mile path that winds around three cones including the giant Vulcan. Head into Albuquerque to shop for souvenir gems at **Skip Maisel's Indian Jewelry** and enjoy an afternoon brew at the **Jones Motor Company**, an Art Moderne gem of a service station that doubles as a beer lovers' brewhouse. Overnight in Gallup at the atmospheric **El Rancho Hotel**.

DAY 5

Enjoy an early-morning drive through the stunning **Petrified National Forest**, then head into Holbrook to gather some souvenir rocks at the **Rainbow Rock Shop**. Take a guided tour of the **Meteor Crater**, one of the best-preserved meteorite impact sites on the planet (tours offered daily at 15 minutes past the hour). Feast on all your fave wheel-flattened delights at the **Roadkill Café** in Seligman; dessert calls for a cone at **Delgadillo's Snow Cap**. Overnight at the largest, oldest, deepest, darkest, quietest motel room in the world, the **Cave Suite at the Grand Canyon Caverns and Inn**.

Wikimedia Commons

DAY 6

Start your day by fueling up on nostalgia at the **Hackberry General Store** in Kingman, Arizona, a Route 66 must-see. Pull over and peek at both the mysterious **Topock Maze** and the incredible **Amboy Crater**. Lunch at the **Baghdad Café** in Newberry Springs. Stroll the **Hollywood Walk of Fame** and sip a late-afternoon martini at the **Formosa Café**. Celebrate your Route 66 journey with funnel cakes and a spin on the carousel at **Santa Monica Pier**.

SUPERNATURAL 66

Route 66 is rich and unique history has birthed a variety of chilling legends, paranormal investigations, and spirited wonders. Ghosts, extreme energy vortexes, portals to the underworld . . . America's byway is packed with so many spine-tingling sites. Follow this six-day itinerary to all the supernatural spots along the Mother Road.

SPRINGFIELD, IL—ST. LOUIS, MO

DAY 1

Your supernatural journey along Route 66 begins in Springfield, Illinois, at the **Dana-Thomas House** (300 E. Lawrence Ave., Springfield, IL; 217-782-6776; dana-thomas.org), a Prairie-style masterpiece of a mansion designed by pioneer architect Frank Lloyd Wright and built for heiress Susan Lawrence Dana in 1902. Dana was a wealthy independent woman—her husband had died two years prior—feminist, suffragist, and one of Springfield's leading social mavens. She lived in her magnificent mansion for about 24 years . . . until she became more and more reclusive. She developed a keen interest in the occult and began to conduct in-home séances. Eventually her fortune dwindled, and Dana was forced to close the difficult-to-maintain main house and move into a small cottage on the grounds. By the 1940s, dementia had taken its toll: Her beloved house and all her belongings were sold to the highest bidder, not long before her death in 1946. Spiritually sensitive visitors to the home report that Dana, dressed in black, still walks the halls, while others have reported eerie voices, mysterious creaking noises, and outright apparitions. Guided tours are offered throughout the day. Don't miss the Wright-designed bowling alley in the basement, where ghosts are known to play a few matches into the wee hours of the night.

Enjoy lunch at one of Springfield's iconic diners: the Maid-Rite Drive-Thru and Cozy Dog Drive In, then make your way to the **Cahokia Mounds State Historic Site**, which is about a 100-mile drive from Springfield.

Cahokia boasted a population of about 20,000 at its peak, but by 1350, this city lay abandoned—and no one knows exactly why. In 1967, archaeologist Melvin Fowler discovered a mass grave containing over 270 bodies while excavating one of Cahokia's 68 preserved mounds. Fowler determined that many of the buried dead were likely sacrificed, possibly drugged and strangled before burial, adding to the mystery of Cahokia and its inhabitants of long ago.

Just west of the main Monks Mound lies a unique sun calendar, created with a series of evenly spaced wooden posts, known as Woodhenge. In August 1987, more than 1,000 people, part of the worldwide "Harmonic Convergence," gathered here on the equinox to watch the sun line up with the wooden posts. Many Native Americans and metaphysical buffs believe that Cahokia is a "power center," i.e., a point of powerful psychic energy. Take a public tour—offered April through November—and soak in some of the site's spiritual energy as you explore the mounds and trails.

Enjoy dinner at the Luna Café in nearby Granite City before settling into St. Louis for the night at the grand Victorian **Lemp Mansion** (322 Demenil Pl., St. Louis, MO; 314-664-8024; lempmansion.com), the most haunted home in St. Louis. Today it's a popular bed-and-breakfast.

John Adam Lemp, who immigrated to St. Louis from Germany in 1838, built an empire out of his prized Falstaff lager beer. By 1870, he had passed his business—and his wealth—on to his son, William, who built Lemp into the largest brewery in St. Louis. But the Lemp empire met a mysterious demise. Frederick Lemp, William's favorite son and heir apparent, died under mysterious circumstances in 1901. Three years later, William shot himself in the head in a bedroom at this very family mansion. William Jr.'s sister, Elsa, who was considered the wealthiest heiress in St. Louis, committed suicide in 1920. In 1922, the magnificent Lemp brewery was sold at auction. William J. Lemp Jr. committed suicide; while his brother, Charles, continued to live at the mansion until he too died of a self-inflicted gunshot wound. Is it any surprise that the mansion is allegedly haunted by restless, unhappy spirits?

The Lemp Mansion is currently an inn and restaurant; tours, both historical and haunted, are offered daily, and it serves as a venue for fabulous murder mystery dinners

and Halloween parties. If you're not fond of ghosts, avoid the former brewery office, located to the left of the main entrance, where William Jr. committed suicide and often returns in spirit, to oversee his fallen empire.

ST. LOUIS, MO—MIAMI, OK

DAY 2

As you head out of St. Louis, take a moment to stop at **8435 Roanoke Dr.** in the lovely suburb of Bel-Nor. It's such a picture-perfect home that it's almost impossible to imagine that in the 1940s, the teenage boy who lived here became possessed by the devil. In late winter 1949, Jesuit priests performed an exorcism on the boy, finally freeing him from Satan's clutch. One of the priests recorded the sordid details in a diary that eventually inspired William Peter Blatty's 1971 book and the subsequent movie adaptation, *The Exorcist*.

You won't want to miss the incredible **Meramec Caverns**, a complex of more than 6,000 surveyed limestone caves and the alleged hideout of Jesse James. The nature-made decor of this cave system will transport you to another, almost alien, underworld.

Take in the brassiere collection and a Bloody Mary at the **Elbow Inn Bar and BBQ in Devils Elbow** then follow the dirt path down to the devilish, difficult-to-navigate bend in the Big Piney River. Locals believed that the bend was worsened by a large boulder that the devil placed there to cause problems. One of the best ways to experience Devils Elbow is by canoe, kayak, or floating your devilish cares away from the comfort of

a floating inner tube. Route 66 Canoe (573-336-2730; rt66canoe.com) in Devils Elbow is the local go-to outfitter for river adventures.

Check into a hotel for the night in Miami. If you're feeling especially brave, take a ride out to rural Quapaw, OK, and try to spot the eerie **Hornet Spooklight**. Considered the scariest tract of Route 66, the so-called "Devil's Promenade" is regularly haunted by this bizarre, flaming orange orb.

MIAMI, OK—AMARILLO, TX

DAY 3

Start your day with a visit to **Fort Reno**, the former US Army cavalry post, where apparitions have been reported since the 1800s. Take a guided tour of the historic fort's 25 remaining buildings, as well as its cemetery, where 70 prisoners of war are interred. Research teams have conducted several investigations here after many reported apparitions over the fort's long, murky history.

Upon arrival in Amarillo, make a beeline to the **Nat** (2705 SW 6th Ave., Amarillo, TX; 806-367-8908), an antiques mall featuring over 100 dealers and home to one of the largest selection of antiques along Route 66. Over the years, this distinct building, built in 1922, has worn many hats—it has been everything from an indoor swimming pool to a dance hall—and ghosts from the past still linger. A psychic was called to investigate the many reports of mysterious whispers and footsteps, only to discover the ghost of a young lady, ready to dance the night away in her white dress complete with blood-stained bodice. A ghostly couple has also been spotted dancing the night away on the former ballroom floor. See if you notice any cold spots—telltale signs that you're not alone—in the upstairs rooms, which once served as a gambling hall.

DAY 4

Take a spooky stroll through **Glenrio Ghost Town**: This tiny town's few inhabitants packed up and left when Route 66 was replaced by Interstate 40 in the 1970s, leaving the area in economic shambles. Glenrio has been a ghost town ever since. It's more than eerie to ramble among the remaining structures, including the Art Moderne–influenced gas station and diner, which have all been affected by the sands of time.

About 222 miles from Glenrio, the **Petroglyph National Monument** stretches along Albuquerque's West Mesa, a volcanic basalt escarpment. The ancestral

Wikimedia Commons

pueblo peoples and early Spanish settlers carved thousands of designs, hundreds of years ago, into the volcanic rocks. While many of the carvings are easy to interpret, others are more complex and remain a mystery. Take a moment to explore the Visitor Center and then park your car at one of the many petroglyph-viewing trailheads and take a hike to see if you can spot the petroglyphs.

Try to time your visit to New Mexico to coincide with the **Burning of Zozobra**. The annual tradition, linked to the Fiestas de Santa Fe, calls for the public burning of a 50-foot-tall marionette effigy every September at Fort Marcy Park. Zozobra, a.k.a. Old Man Gloom, has been built anew each year since the first event in 1924. To burn Zozobra is to burn all your worries and troubles of the previous year away. Can't make the actual burning? Write down your worry on a slip of paper and leave it in the "gloom box" found in the offices of the *Santa Fe Reporter* at 132 E. Marcy St. in the weeks leading up to the burn: All the written-down worries in the gloom box will be placed at Zozobra's feet and fed to the flames of time along with Zozobra himself.

Check into the fancy boutique **Hotel Parq** (806 Central Ave. SE, Albuquerque, NM; 888-796-7277; hotelparqcentral.com) one of the grandest hotels in Albuquerque—and likely one of the most haunted, too. That's because the building was not always a hotel: Built as a hospital for railroad employees, it was renamed Memorial Hospital in the 1980s and switched to operating as a psychiatric asylum. After repeated reports of apparitions and mysterious noises, a paranormal investigation group visited the hotel in 2011 and confirmed that there's unusually spooky and frequent activity. Cap off your evening with a visit to the hotel's rooftop lounge for some 1920s-era cocktails: The bar is aptly named "The Apothecary Lounge" and comes complete with vintage medicine bottles and stunning panoramic views of the mountains and downtown skyline.

The truly brave will want to venture out to the visit the **Mine Shaft Tavern**, located about 45 miles from the Hotel Parq, for a nightcap. It's no surprise that this popular tavern, one of the oldest in Santa Fe County, built as an after-work hangout for the local miners, is haunted by those who never made it out of the shaft. Orbs often appear in photos taken here. Head to the restroom and gaze into the mirror: There have been several reports of patrons seeing another face, staring over their shoulder, in the reflection.

ALBUQUERQUE, NM—SEDONA, AZ

DAY 5

When was the last time you connected with a swirling center of sacred energy? Sedona is not only home to some of the most beautiful vistas in the world. It's also a place where mysterious cosmic forces emanate from rock vortexes, where soul seekers come to be inspired, recharged, and reconnected with the spiritual. Although all of Sedona is considered a powerful field of radiating energy, there are specific sites where the flow is more intense. **Sedona Red Rock Tours** (928-282-0993; sedonaredrocktours.com) is one of the few companies authorized by the US Forest Service to take visitors out to the sites that boast the most potent energy. Immerse yourself in Sedona's unparalleled natural beauty while also soaking in some transformative vortex power.

Alternatively, drive out to the trailheads of Sedona's four main vortexes—**Cathedral Rock, Boynton Canyon, Bell Rock Vortex, and Airport Vortex**—and discover them on your own. Visit the Sedona Visitor Center (331 Forest Rd., Sedona, AZ; 928-282-7722; sedonachamber.com/visitor-center) to pick up detailed trail maps. Whether you take a tour or take a hike, be prepared to rock your world as you journey amidst the red rocks.

SEDONA, AZ—NEEDLES, CA

DAY 6

Your supernatural journey along Route 66 ends at what the local Mohave people believe is the spiritual portal to the afterlife. **Topock Maze** is a 600-plus-year-old, 15-acre maze of a geoglyph, where bad souls tend to get lost in the ancient, intricate pathways, while good souls find the door to a peaceful eternity. Though you can't walk the maze in search of the mysterious portal—the maze is fenced off for protection from vandals—it's an incredible, supernatural site to see.

#ROUTE66TOP100
#SELFIECHALLENGE

Only die-hard Mother Road lovers will have what it takes to complete the Route 66 Selfie Challenge. Snap a selfie at each of our top 100 picks for the best on the byway and tag your posts with the hashtags #Route66Top100 #SelfieChallenge.

1. Snap a selfie at the official "Begin Historic Illinois US Route 66" sign *Chicago, IL*
2. Coffee-sipping selfie at Lou Mitchell's Restaurant and Bakery *Chicago, IL*
3. Fried chicken leg biting selfie at Dell Rhea's Chicken Basket *Willowbrook, IL*
4. Selfie standing or parked at the finish line of the Car Racing Experience at the Route 66 Raceway *Elwood, IL*
5. Selfie amid the tall prairie grasses of Midewin National Tallgrass Prairie. Bonus point if you capture a buffalo in the distance *Wilmington, IL*
6. Selfie standing next to the Gemini Giant *Wilmington, IL*
7. Selfie standing at the side rear passenger door of Bob Waldmire's 1972 VW microbus at the Route 66 Association Hall of Fame and Museum *Pontiac, IL*
8. Selfie near a tapped tree (seasonal) or licking a maple leaf lollipop at Funks Grove Pure Maple Sirup *Shirley, IL*
9. Selfie standing or parked on the Auburn Brick Road *Auburn, IL*
10. Selfie standing at the doorstep of Abraham Lincoln's historic home *Springfield, IL*
11. Selfie biting into a cozy dog at the Cozy Dog Drive In *Springfield, IL*
12. Phosphate-sipping selfie at Doc's Soda Fountain *Girard, IL*
13. Selfie standing before the main screen of the Sky View Drive-In *Litchfield, IL*
14. Counterside, coffee-sipping selfie at Ariston Café *Litchfield, IL*
15. Selfie with a bunny buddy at Henry's Rabbit Ranch *Stauton, IL*
16. Selfie standing before Monk's Mound in Cahokia Mounds State Historic Site *Collinsville, IL*

17. Selfie standing below the World's Largest Catsup Bottle *Collinsville, IL*
18. Selfie standing below the iconic neon sign at Luna Café *Granite City, IL*
19. Selfie at the Chain of Rocks Bridge's halfway point *Granite City, IL /St. Louis, MO*
20. Selfie with the Gateway Arch soaring in the background *St. Louis, MO*
21. Selfie on the front steps the Old Courthouse *St. Louis, MO*
22. Selfie with a custard cone or sundae at Ted Drewes Frozen Custard *St. Louis, MO*
23. Selfie standing before Union Pacific Big Boy Number 4006 at the National Museum of Transportation *St. Louis, MO*
24. Selfie capturing the adobe rooftop of the Big Chief Roadhouse *Wildwood, MO*
25. Selfie standing in front of Meramec Caverns' Stage Curtain *Sullivan, MO*
26. Selfie standing in the doorway of a motor cottage at the Wagon Wheel Motel *Cuba, MO*
27. Selfie below the iconic Munger Moss Motel roadside sign *Devils Elbow, MO*
28. Selfie in front of the fudge selection at the Uranus Fudge Factory *Uranus, MO*
29. Selfie standing at the historical marker Old Stagecoach Stop *Waynesville, MO*
30. Selfie standing below the Gillioz Theatre marquee *Springfield, MO*
31. Selfie standing beside the vintage Best Western sign at the Best Western Route 66 Rail Haven. Bonus point for a selfie taken tucked into the Elvis Room's Chevy bed *Springfield, MO*
32. Selfie standing near a cannon at Wilson's Creek National Battlefield Park *Republic, MO*
33. Selfie sitting in one of the chairs outside the entrance of Boots Court Motel *Carthage, MO*
34. Selfie in front of the garage at the Bonnie and Clyde Hideout *Joplin, MO*
35. Selfie with Tow Mater at the Kan-O-Tex Service Station *Galena, KS*
36. Snap a selfie with your feet on two different states and a hand on yet

another at the Three State Marker (Downstream Boulevard and 118th Street) in *Quapaw, OK*. Bonus 100 points if you manage to capture a photo of the Hornet Spooklight.

37. Selfie standing beside the vintage pumps at Allen's Conoco Fillin' Station *Commerce, OK*
38. Selfie standing under the marquee of the Coleman Theatre *Miami, OK*
39. Selfie atop a motorcycle, inside or in front of the Vintage Iron Motorcycle Museum *Miami, OK*
40. Selfie standing roadside on the slim Ribbon Road *Miami, OK*
41. Selfie standing beside the Predicta at the National Rod and Custom Car Hall *Afton, OK*
42. Selfie hugging the tallest totem pole at Ed Galloway's Totem Pole Park *Chelsea, OK*
43. Selfie standing inside the open jaws of the Blue Whale of Catoosa *Catoosa, OK*
44. Selfie standing under the marquee of the Circle Cinema *Tulsa, OK*
45. Selfie standing before the outdoor mural of a guitar-strumming Guthrie at the Woody Guthrie Center *Tulsa, OK*
46. Selfie standing below the Cain's Ballroom Dancing marquee at Cain's Ballroom *Tulsa, OK*
47. Selfie standing beside Avery's Model T at Cyrus Avery Centennial Plaza *Tulsa, OK*
48. Selfie standing at the start of the Rock Creek Bridge *Sapulpa, OK*
49. Selfie standing beside the Rock Café's distinctive façade *Stroud, OK*
50. Selfie capturing the Arcadia Round Barn in the background *Arcadia, OK*
51. Selfie sipping a soda at POPS Soda Ranch *Arcadia, OK*
52. Selfie standing at the door of the First Public Schoolhouse in Oklahoma Territory *Edmond, OK*
53. Selfie capturing the oversize milk bottle atop the Milk Bottle Grocery *Oklahoma City, OK*
54. Selfie standing in front of the chapel at Fort Reno *El Reno, OK*
55. Selfie with a smokehouse BBQ sandwich from Jigg's Smokehouse *Clinton, OK*

56. Selfie standing beside the retro fuel pumps at Conoco Tower Station *Shamrock, TX*

57. Selfie with the Palo Duro Canyon as a backdrop *Canyon, TX*

58. Selfie beside the giant cow statue at Big Texan Steak Ranch *Amarillo, TX*

59. Selfie with your favorite Caddy at Cadillac Ranch *Amarillo, TX*

60. Selfie standing beside the Route 66 midpoint sign at the Midpoint Café *Adrian, TX*

61. Selfie standing before a long-abandoned building in the Glenrio ghost town. Bonus point if you capture a tumbleweed in your selfie *Glenrio, TX*

62. Selfie standing below the Blue Swallow Motel's neon sign *Tucumcari, NM*

63. Selfie diving into the big, Blue Hole *Santa Rosa, NM*

64. Selfie standing in front of the entrance of historic San Miguel Chapel *Santa Fe, NM*

65. Selfie standing beside the Southwest-style hearth at La Fonda on the Plaza *Santa Fe, NM*

66. Selfie of burning Zozobra or a selfie of your letter to Zozobra *Santa Fe, NM*

67. Selfie standing in front of the central Trading Post *Kewa Pueblo, NM*

68. Selfie of your reflection in the haunted mirror at the Mine Shaft Tavern. Bonus 100 points if you capture a ghost *Madrid, NM*

69. Sing-along selfie recording your car singing "America the Beautiful" on the Musical Road of Tijeras *Tijeras, NM*

70. Beer-sipping selfie at Jones Motor Company *Albuquerque, NM*

71. Selfie imitating the pose of the Madonna of the Trail *Albuquerque, NM*

72. Selfie standing below the marquee of KiMo Theater *Albuquerque, NM*

73. Selfie with your fave piece of jewelry at Skip Maisel's *Albuquerque, NM*

74. Rattlesnake selfie at the American International Rattlesnake Museum *Albuquerque, NM*

75. Selfie sitting at the star-shape fountain in the courtyard of Los Poblanos Historic Inn and Organic Farm *Albuquerque, NM*

76. Selfie with a petroglyph from the Petroglyph National Monument *Albuquerque, NM*

77. Selfie with one of the statues in Sky City's central plaza *Pueblo, NM*

78. Selfie in the lobby of the El Rancho Hotel *Gallup, NM*

79. Selfie with a petrified log from the Petrified Forest National Park *Petrified Forest, AZ*

80. Selfie with your favorite rock at the Rainbow Rock Shop *Holbrook, AZ*

81. Selfie standing beside a wigwam at the Wigwam Motel *Holbrook, AZ*

82. Selfie standin' on the famous corner *Winslow, AZ*

83. Selfie with the Meteor Crater as a backdrop *Winslow, AZ*

84. Selfie peering into a telescope at Lowell Observatory *Flagstaff, AZ*

85. Selfie sliding down a rock (seasonal) or standing on a rock at the Slide Rock State Park *Sedona, AZ*

86. Selfie at the entrance to the Williams Depot *Williams, AZ*

87. Selfie pretending to be a mannequin outside of the Rusty Bolt *Seligman, AZ*

88. Selfie with the giant T. rex outside the Grand Canyon Caverns and Inn *Peach Springs, AZ*

89. Selfie with your favorite vintage car in front of the Hackberry General Store *Kingman, AZ*

90. Selfie with a burro *Oatman, AZ*

91. Selfie with the Old Trails Bridge in the background *Topock, AZ*

92. Selfie standing before the historical marker at the Topock Maze *Needles, CA*

93. Selfie standing atop a dune at Kelso Dunes *San Bernardino County, CA*

94. Selfie standing at the edge of the Amboy Crater *San Bernardino County, CA*

95. Selfie sipping coffee counterside at the Bagdad Café *Newberry Springs, CA*
96. Selfie amid the bottle trees at Elmer's Bottle Tree Ranch *Oro Grande, CA*
97. Selfie by the gravestone of your favorite star forever interred in the Hollywood Forever Cemetery *Hollywood, CA*
98. Selfie with your hands placed in the prints of your favorite star along the Hollywood Walk of Fame *Hollywood, CA*
99. Selfie sipping a martini barside at Formosa Café *West Hollywood, CA*
100. Selfie at the end of the trail sign on Santa Monica Pier *Santa Monica, CA*

INDEX

T

U

V

W

Y

Z

ABOUT THE AUTHOR

Amy Bizzarri is a freelance writer with a focus on family adventures and outdoor fun. She has a keen interest in Chicago history and is the author of *111 Places in Chicago That You Must Not Miss* and *Discovering Vintage Chicago*. Route 66 holds a special place in her heart, and you might just find her on the road, hiking the Petrified Forest, climbing the Amboy Crater, or diving into the Blue Hole of Santa Rosa.